Complete Guide to Coaching Women's Basketball

Complete Guide to Coaching Women's Basketball

Dorothy A. Guiliani

Parker Publishing Company, Inc.   West Nyack, New York

Library of Congress Cataloging in Publication Data

Guiliani, Dorothy A., 1942-
    Complete guide to coaching women's basketball.

    Includes index.
    1. Basketball for women—Coaching.   I. Title.
GV886.G84   796.32'38   81-16790
ISBN 0-13-160465-1   AACR2

Printed in the United States of America

WHAT THIS COMPLETE GUIDE
WILL DO FOR YOU

Complete Guide to Coaching Women's Basketball gives you a detailed plan that includes every conceivable obstacle, requirement and aspect of a season. In the plan are designs for stat sheets; guides for putting together a staff of students with specific jobs; a progression of offenses and defenses that teach players to do some of their own coaching on the floor, eliminating wasted timeouts for minor adjustments; suggestions for adapting team personnel if the flu bug hits or a rash of injuries occurs; specific factors to look for in tryouts; and multipurpose drills to take advantage of time, that precious commodity. You will discover how to begin a season with a basic workable offense and develop it as the year progresses. Plays and strategy will be available for use by your team to take advantage of every aspect of the rules, atmosphere and opponents' attitudes. An entire season that begins one month before tryouts and ends one month after the final game is mapped out in detail.

The Complete Guide shows you how, by establishing the specific role of each of your players, you can set out with your schedule of work, ranging from the basic basketball play to all situations that will keep you competitive, and reach the end of the season where you have enhanced, polished and refined each concept you have presented. By the time tournaments begin, you will have taught your team not just some offense and defense but rather the game of basketball.

The Complete Guide presents the Total Approach to a basketball season that gives you a well-paced learning and playing schedule. It gives high productivity and efficiency through the use of all of your players and all of their skills. You learn to concentrate on what your team is doing by preparing them for a diversity of opponents, instead of running around the countryside collecting volumes of material about each opponent. It will decidedly reduce your scouting time to a point where a newspaper article will often suffice. If you know the size, basic defenses and outstanding personnel of your opponents, you can tell where the attack areas will be and whom your team must stop. You spend a season working on the development of your team, not running each practice as a hurry-up stopgap measure against every specific opponent you have. Your Total Approach will have made them thinking players, not just acting or reacting players.

The Complete Guide provides not just an offensive or defensive philosophy and strategy but also drills gaining maximum use of each minute of practice; aggressive, positive special situation plays that lead to quick, easy baskets; simple but thorough statistics forms that anyone can use and that provide you the information you need to coach effectively. You will read of strategy to use throughout the game that allows you to direct the pace of the game, counteracting your opponent's game plan and actually turning it to your advantage.

In *The Complete Guide* you will find an offense that is workable for a variety of playing levels. The mobile mid-post can be used in elementary school programs because it teaches fundamentals such as passing and penetration to the basket, and it accommodates a variety of skill levels. Its shot options include simple setup jump shots and complex movements that depend on timing. It has been used successfully with post-college players because it creates a number of offensive attacks from different locations on the floor. The overload offense is particularly good for teaching young players strategy and floor balance at the same time.

A multiplicity of defenses—zone, man-to-man and pressure—is explained and illustrated in detail. From simple, basic positioning to complex, moving adjustments, you will be able to find the suitable stopper your team can use. Not only is the strength of each defense explained but also the weaknesses that your players can be taught to attack when they have the ball.

The Guide consistently explains the "why" of the game, not just the "how." It will assist you in forming your explanations to your players concerning methods of approach to developing offenses, defenses, and special plays.

While most basketball books are content to explain the technical end of the game, *The Guide* provides the strategic part. All of us can use development in strategy but are usually provided only with on-the-job training. Here you will find specific situations pinpointing what you should do. For all of those nail-biting times, even overtimes, you are given specific instruction. If you're tied, down by two, up by two, in foul trouble, and many more given circumstances, the necessary steps to victory are fully explained.

Your record will reveal the difference in your approach to the game. Without the plan, our team played .500 ball. With the plan in the very first year, our team went undefeated. The next year with only three players—not starters—returning from the undefeated season, we once again finished unbeaten. With that kind of result, two consecutive undefeated seasons, it is obvious to see that *The Complete Guide* gives you a total approach that Works!

Dorothy A. Guiliani

ACKNOWLEDGMENTS

This book is the result of years of fun, work and study. Without the efforts of every coach and player I know who has been involved in Dr. Naismith's game, this book would not have been possible. The contents are an accumulation of the vast opportunities to observe, try and study each aspect of the game which, for me, began in pickup playground games with some of the boy's varsity players in Iron Mountain, Michigan when I was a child. Since then, because the philosophies and strategies of the game fascinated me, I have read every basketball book—fiction and nonfiction—in the libraries of the towns where I have lived. There have been too many for me to identify where specific information came from, but each has made a contribution to my basketball education. I thank each author. Too, my gratitude goes out to every play-by-play announcer and game analyst of all the many radio and television broadcasts that I have enjoyed. Their genius has also placed entries in my intellectual file.

The opportunity to coach was given to me by Sandy Clark, former Athletic Director and Coach at St. Joseph Academy. For that chance I will always be grateful. For her continued support, I thank Jean Einerson, friend and former Athletic Director and Coach at St. Joseph Academy. To my parents, Louis and Anne Guiliani, I express my heartfelt thanks for enduring my athletic interests and involvement when it wasn't socially acceptable, across the country—and especially in our neighborhood. And finally, thank you to my players who understood what "team" was all about; it is to them I dedicate this book.

Dorothy A. Guiliani

TABLE OF CONTENTS

9

1

PLANNING THE COMPLETE WOMEN'S BASKETBALL SEASON

Coaching basketball can be a full-time job. Ask any NBA or college coach. As a high school coach, there are too many other responsibilities that prevent coaching from becoming a full-time job. Your teaching abilities are your prime reason for being hired in a school system, or should have been, and as you surely will tell your team, you must keep up your primary responsibilities. Your teaching affects far more students, and they must come first. Yet when basketball season begins, it seems there is nothing else in the world but practice and games. If you are not at either one, your mind is still on basketball. You eat, sleep, dream it. The total approach will make your season much lighter. It will give you time for something other than basketball.

One measure of determining how much your coaching affects your teaching in terms of time consumption is to honestly appraise your classes. What are you offering? If you teach physical education, are you simply throwing out a ball and telling the students to play? If you teach science, social studies, or literature, do you increase self-study and project assignments that require less of your time? Your players judge you by your action. If they realize that everything is basketball, they too will assume that attitude and in so doing neglect

their studies and miss one of the most important components
of their education. To avoid making this error, plan your entire
season before it begins.

SETTING A SCHEDULE

Long before a season begins the game schedule is prepared. This generally occurs the previous spring, particularly
if you are a member of a league or conference. A few
nonconference games are added after the conference has made
up its schedule. As far as the conference schedule is concerned, you have no voice in it. However, the nonconference
games should be of your choosing and should be used as a tool
in preparing your team for its conference season and as a
method of experimenting during the season. Work with your
athletic director and explain what you are trying to accomplish with the nonconference games.

One of these games should be scheduled to begin your
season. Choose a team that you have a very high probability of
defeating. It will probably be a smaller school who would like
to run with the "big girls." However, don't make it such a
mismatch that neither of you can benefit from it. Midway
through the season, schedule a team that has a similar
approach to the game that one of your strongest foes has. If
your weakness has been against a man-to-man defense, find
an opponent whose reputation has been for using man-to-
man. If you have difficulty in breaking presses, find a pressing
team. Most coaches have favorite defenses and try to use them
each year. If you use a stack, it is probably because you know
it, believe in it, and have had success with it. You become
known for it. Know what your area opponents use and set
your nonconference games on the basis of that knowledge. It
will give you an opportunity to try a variety of offenses or
defenses to meet the problems you encounter in your conference. Toward the end of the regular season, schedule a
game with a team that has many looks, not just a fast-break,
not just a zone defense team. This multiple approach team
will help you prepare for the tournaments you enter. This

game, too, should be one which you have a high probability of
winning. A strong positive effort before a tournament is a
must to prepare your team psychologically.

GATHERING EQUIPMENT FOR PRACTICE AND GAMES

At least a month before tryouts begin, check all of the
equipment you will be using for practice and games. Notice I
did not say have the equipment checked; I said check it. If you
are employed by a large company and you are part of
management, delegation is a necessity. However, a basketball
team is not a large company. You probably have fifteen girls,
one manager and maybe an assistant coach, and if you are
really fortunate, a trainer. This is a small group who will be
involved in a highly emotional atmosphere and too much
delegation from day one can cause one large problem: Who is
in charge? If you delegate all of the responsibilities other than
the actual coaching, you have too many people making decisions affecting your team. It is impossible to do everything
yourself, but you must establish that you are the coach and
have the position of responsibility. Each of the people on your
team has a role to fulfill. At the same time, each of them must
realize she is accountable to you. While you will delegate
various jobs to the people on your staff, they must never
question that you are in charge. If they are left on their own,
at what point do these people determine they must confer with
you concerning any actions they may take? They must keep
you informed as to what is being done and why they are doing
it. If the trainer needs supplies for the first aid box, she cannot
just go out and buy them. That act needs your approval. The
tone you set at the very beginning of the season will last all
through the year. Make certain that all of your people know
you are in charge.

Starting with equipment and training supplies, check all
areas with the people involved. Choose a manager as soon as
possible if you don't have one returning. It is a responsible
position. If you have many people to choose from, look for
maturity as a prime factor in your decision. Have your

manager work with you to see that the balls are clean and filled with air. At the initial inspection make it clear what you expect for the remainder of the season. Thereafter, don't assume the job is done. Make periodic checks, and a pat on the back will ensure that it will be done.

Your trainer can be one of the most important people in your organization. If you have a student trainer, the job may be considered by her to be the primary responsibility she has. If you allow her free reign, you will have a team that may look like the walking wounded; everyone with some kind of bandage or tape job. You obviously want your injured players taken care of; injuries need attention, but there has to be an attitude of preventive training or you could find yourself with more players in the training room than on the floor at the start of practice. Many athletes, and especially girls with a high level of sensitivity, use an injury as a means of gaining attention. Make sure your trainer knows where you stand on attitude towards the care and attention of injuries.

ORGANIZING A STAFF: STATS PEOPLE

Statistics are a vital part of your overall plan. After much experimenting, I have arrived at three forms for game use that give me what I need. That means you will need three reliable people who are somewhat knowledgeable about the game. These three people must realize that they have very important jobs; and that their dependability is essential. Because in all likelihood they are students, your stats forms must be clear and simple. If they are too complex, you won't get the information you will come to depend on.

The three forms I use are the shot chart, rebounds, and plus and minus chart.

The shot chart is used for each quarter; if you stretch it to halves it becomes too messy to remain accurate (Diagram 1-1).

It is imperative at halftime that you know who is controlling the boards, specifically and on both teams. If the opponent is getting too many offensive rebounds, an adjustment must be made in personnel, position or defensive coverage. If

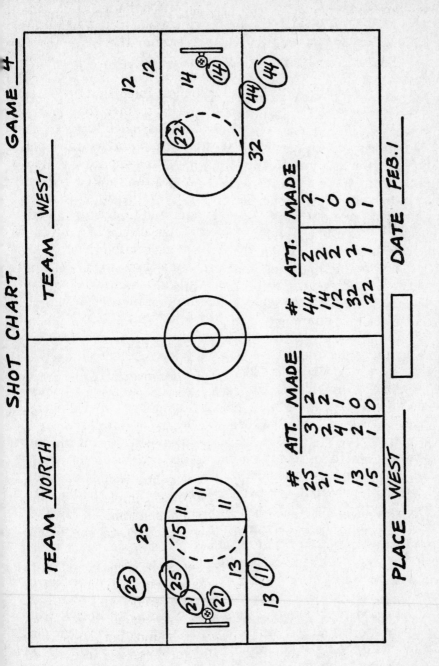

Diagram 1-1

you are going to give your opponent three chances at the basket each time down, you might as well pack your gear and go home (Diagram 1-2).

The plus and minus chart is valuable after a game in determining what areas need attention in practice. It can also tell you at halftime if turnovers are deciding the game. If you are pressing, the Interception/Steal column should tell you if you are having any success. If your opponent is pressing, the Bad Passes and Lost Dribble columns will tell you where your problems are. Multiple travelling calls against one of your players might tell you it may not be her night and someone else will have to do the job. Even though you are watching the game and are aware of the mistakes being made, there is nothing like a black and white report to confirm your suspicions (Diagram 1-3, page 20).

One of the three statisticians should be appointed head of the stats staff and be given the responsibility of recapping all stats at the end of the game.

My game summary form looks like Diagram 1-4 (page 21).

Finally for the files, I have individual stats summaries, as in Diagram 1-5 (page 22).

I keep individual stats files for three reasons. At mid-season I give the stats to the players and point out where they are doing a good job and where they need work. I tell them not to compare with others because each is contributing in her own way, with her own strengths, and that this is not a contest. They know they will receive their year-end stats and should compare mid-year to year-end to look for improvement. The only time I would not give out mid-season stats is if I had all close games or if there are injuries preventing play and not everyone had gotten into at least two games where they had a chance to prove themselves under game conditions. The only stat I post in the gym for everyone to see is free-throw percentages. I have the manager keep a record of all attempts in practice and combine those with game attempts. All players are listed. It's one factor all players can work on and competition to be on the top of the list helps the entire team.

With the growth in women's sports, more colleges and

REBOUNDS

Place _____ Date _____ Game _____

North

North Player	Qtr. 1 D	Qtr. 1 O	Qtr. 2 D	Qtr. 2 O	Qtr. 3 D	Qtr. 3 O	Qtr. 4 D	Qtr. 4 O
25	11	1	111		11		111	
21	111	11	11		111		111	
11	1							
14	111			1	11	1		1
13			1	1	1			
15					11			
24	11							
33						1		
30			1	1			11	1
10								
35			1				11	
20							11	1
Total	11 / 3		8 / 3		8 / 3		11 / 1	

West

West Player	Qtr. 1 D	Qtr. 1 O	Qtr. 2 D	Qtr. 2 O	Qtr. 3 D	Qtr. 3 O	Qtr. 4 D	Qtr. 4 O
14	111		1111		1111		111	
24	1			1		11		11
22				1				11
34				1				
10								
44	11		1		111		11	
32				1				
12								
30	111		11111	1	111	1	11	
20								
42	1		1	1			11	
40				1				
Total	9 / 1		13 / 5		12 / 3		14 / 2	

Diagram 1-2

PLUS AND MINUS CHART

Place _____ Date _____ Game _____

Player	Assist	Interception Steal	Blocked Shots	Jump Ball	Lost Dribble	Bad Pass	Travelling	Line Violation
25			11	11		1		1
21	1	111	111	1111	1		11	111
11	111	11			11		111	1
14								
13	1					11		
15	11	1		11	1		1	1
24				11		11		
33								
30	1			1				
10	1				1	1	1	
35				11				1
20								
Total	8	6	5	14	5	6	7	7

Diagram 1-3

GAME SUMMARY

Place _____ Date _____ Game _____

SCORE

	Home	Guest

FG% [ ]

FT% [ ]

Player	Pts.	FG AH	FG Made	FT AH	FT Made	Rbs.	Ast.	Int./ Steals	Turn-overs
TOTAL									

Diagram 1-4

21

INDIVIDUAL HISTORY CHART

Player _____   Year _____

Opponent	Points	Rebounds	Assists	Interceptions Steals	Turnovers	FG		FT	
						AH	made	AH	made
Total									

Diagram 1-5

universities are offering athletic scholarships. If I can help one of our girls to receive a grant, I want to be ready. The individual stats are kept from year to year for each girl. Should any inquiries be made, I can find them easily.

Finally, if for some reason I should not return to the school to coach the following year, I want to leave a record for my successor. She should not have to start from scratch. The individual stats along with an evaluation of strengths and weaknesses of each player is waiting for her use. If I walked into a new school setting with players completely unknown to me, I would appreciate having a place to start.

PREPARING A SPECIFIC PRACTICE PLAN

Your most important preseason work is preparing your practice plan. Most state athletic associations dictate specific opening dates when you can begin practice. From that date until your first game is the time when you put a team together. You are taking a diverse group of skills, ability, talent and attitude and blending them into a team effort.

Every minute of preseason must be planned. The following is the practice timetable I have recently used:

Nov. 7—Tryouts

Warm-ups—15 min.
Dribble-pivot-pass drill—20 min.
Air-Bounce combo drill—20 min.
4-corner pass w/lay-up—20 min.
Tapping drill—20 min.
Dribble one-on-one, defender has no hands—20 min.

Nov. 8—Tryouts

Warm-ups—15 min.
Three player weave—20 min.
Air-Bounce combo w/defense—20 min.
Star drill—20 min.
High post, split—no defense—20 min.

Continuous shooting lines—20 min.

Nov. 9—Tryouts

Warm-ups—15 min.
One-on-one—20 min.
Two-on-two—20 min.
Aggression line-up—20 min.
Pass around 2-1-2 zone—20 min.
Scrimmage—20 min.

Nov. 10—3:10 to 5:00

Warm-ups/conditioning—15 min.
Drills—pass, dribble—20 min.
Defense; man-to-man principles—40 min.
Offense-overload

Nov. 11

Warm-ups/conditioning—15 min.
Drills—pivot and rebounding—20 min.
Defense—zone press-2-2-1—40 min.
Offense—overload

Nov. 13

Warm-ups/conditioning—15 min.
Drills—passing—20 min.
Defense 2-2-1 zone press—40 min.
Offense—overload

Nov. 14

Warm-ups/conditioning—15 min.
Drills—pass, dribble—20 min.
Defense—3-1-1 zone press—30 min.
Offense—overload
Shooting—10 min.

Nov. 15

Warm-ups/conditioning—15 min.
Drills—rebounding—20 min.
Defense—3-1-1 zone press—30 min.
Offense—overload—30 min.
Free-throw instruction—20 min.

Nov. 16

Warm-ups/conditioning—15 min.
Drills—pass, dribble—20 min.
Defense—fall back from press—20 min.
Offense—add challenge—30 min.
Specials—out-of-bounds—25 min.

Nov. 17

Warm-ups/conditioning—10 min.
Shooting—quick jump—20 min.
1:50 Defense—pull together—20 min.
Offense—high post—30 min.
Specials—jump ball—30 min.

Nov. 18

Warm-ups/conditioning—10 min.
Drills—pass, dribble—20 min.
1:50 Defense—set zone—30 min.
Offense—overload—30 min.
Shooting—20 min.

Nov. 21

Warm-ups/conditioning—15 min.
Talk on blending O and D—30 min.
1:25   (check their knowledge w/play situations)
Scrimmage—30 min.
Shooting—10 min. *15*

Nov. 22

First game

Our organization states that you must have ten practices on ten different days between opening day and the first game. We had twelve and used each minute.

The above practice plan was prepared without knowledge of who would be on the team. It is general enough to make specific detailed plans as the players and their skills permit, but yet it states what must be accomplished before game one. Don't post it for the team to read. Take them along one practice at a time.

STAYING WITH THE PLAN

As practice begins, if you have a day when nothing seems to go right, stay with the schedule anyway. The players may seem lethargic (how many days consecutively can you stay fresh?) something may have happened in school to set a somber mood, and—hey, coach, it may be you. Plug along. Tomorrow's another day and you'll make it.

If you have a thirty-minute block set for offense and no one is catching on, at the end of that period go on to your next scheduled point. Don't belabor the point. I find that any time the majority of the group doesn't understand what I am presenting, the fault is with me. Find another way to explain it another day.

As you can see, the schedule always follows the same pattern, warm-ups, drills, defense, offense, and specials. This is simply because I stress fundamentals and defense. I believe they are the major reason for winning. If you are not throwing the ball away and you are stopping your opponent from scoring, you don't need high percentage shooters or a fancy, complex offense. I therefore keep those two areas early in the practice while the players still have high energy levels.

REVIEWING OFFENSES AND DEFENSES

In the month preceding the start of practice, review the various offenses and defenses that you know best. This close to the season is no time to try to learn something totally new for use this year. Summer is the time for that. This is review time. If you feel comfortable with a stack offense, use it. If basic zone offenses are your forte, use them. Three weeks before the season is not the time to initially investigate zone presses. There are too many intricacies to try to learn and remember or master zone presses in three weeks. If you have ten to twelve hours a day to study them, it would be possible but you probably have only two or three and then that much time isn't available to you daily. And remember, if you don't know it, you can't fake it. It's not like a classroom where you can give them a study period while you catch up on your studying. Every minute you waste in preseason is going to catch up with you during the season.

While coaches and players have separate and different roles in the game, in one respect they are the same. They are individuals from March to November and a team from November to March. The players should be working on individual skills in the summer. The coaches should do their learning during the summer. That's the time to take a month with a new book and totally break down an offense, literally step-by-step on the floor. Know what you are teaching the team; don't learn it with them.

PLANNING TRYOUTS

Beyond any question, to me the only bad aspect of the game is tryouts. If there were any way to get around them, someone would have thought of it by now. They are, however, inevitable, and you have to try to make the best of it. They should be exciting—the thought of Christmas gift opening could be analagous—but they have never struck me in that way. Tryouts mark the beginning of another exciting season, yet, turn out to be the worst part of the season. You start with many and have to tell people that they aren't good enough; that is never a pleasurable task.

In tryouts you will have girls who have no chance of making the team. The skills just aren't there and yet it is only fair that you look at them. They must have their opportunity to try, so as difficult as it may seem, keep an open mind.

There are obviously some players who will be returning from last year's team. If they were starters or strong subs use them as group leaders and demonstrators. Remember that every team needs leaders and here is a place to start developing them. On the first day of tryouts, the seniors run everything. Every drill, warm-up, and game situation is directed and demonstrated by the seniors. If you include freshmen in your tryouts, introduce the seniors by giving a brief summary of the contributions they have made in the past. Treated as mature, experienced people, they will respond accordingly and the underclassmen have someone to emulate. In the preseason plan you read earlier, there are three days devoted to tryouts. On all of those days, multipurpose drills are used. Those drills give you a better opportunity to see a girl's overall ability yet determine her strengths and weaknesses. Can she pass accurately, cut to the opposite side of the floor, receive the ball on the run and move to the basket? In one drill you judge passing, receiving, speed, depth perception, and the ability to follow directions.

I don't believe in a long tryout period. Preseason is too short, considering how much work must be done by the first game, to spend half of that period observing people's skills. Further, if you keep too many that will eventually be cut, you must continuously be working them into your drills. If you just keep them and they spend their time in practice standing on the sidelines observing while what you consider your best ten are doing the work, you really have an absurd situation. You are eventually going to have to decide who is on the team. Spare yourself—and above all, the girls—the extended agony. Decide and get on with preparing for the season.

2

ACTIVATING THE WOMEN'S TEAM IMMEDIATELY

MAKING YOUR PLANS KNOWN: THE PRESEASON MEETING

We have a preseason meeting in a classroom, not the gym. Many coaches feel, and I agree, that the classroom is the best place for the meeting because you want a listening, not playing, environment. During this meeting we discuss what we are looking for in terms of skill, ability, and attitude, what we expect. All of the basketball coaches are present and anyone who will be a part of the team, trainers and managers alike, is expected to attend. We state all of the rules and stress that they will be enforced.

Small 3″ by 5″ index cards are given each girl, and we ask for the following information:

Name: Grade Level:

Address:

Phone:

Height, weight:

Grade Point Average:

Previous injuries:

Extracurricular activities:

We need the phone number for curfew calls on nights before a game. We ask for grades earned to impress upon the girls that they are students first, and we make clear that studies are their first priority. Previous injuries are reported to the trainers for preventive purposes. Attendance at all practice is required and if another activity will cause a conflict the player must make a choice. If she has difficulty in making that choice, I help her. A 5'10" freshman asked if she could ski on weekends, missing Sunday afternoon practices and still be on the team. I told her that wasn't possible. She then expressed a strong liking for skiing to which I replied she could ski Monday through Saturday in addition to Sunday. Special rules exist for no one. Team concept cannot be stressed if you have a variety of rules for certain people.

At the preseason meeting I always give a talk that emphasizes the same ideas; different words and examples are used. My preseason talk is one of the few speeches that I spend a good bit of time preparing. It is vital that your ideas about the sport and your philosophy of the game be made clear. With this speech you will set the tone of the season. Your ideas must be presented in a precise manner, seriously, with a purpose, yet have some light moments. All within a half hour the prospective players must gain the impression that you are dedicated, yet not totally consumed by the sport. If the speech is too long, they may interpret you as another teacher giving a lecture. If it is too serious, you will sound sermonizing. Make sure before they leave the room that they know you are human, have feelings, and have the capacity to apply yourself to a given objective, yet can enjoy yourself too.

Tryouts always seem to be a disaster even when they go well. I have found this to be true even with my highly organized system. Other coaches and teachers who have observed the tryout period disagree with me, so it may just be me. At any rate, they are not my favorite days, regardless of how positive I try to be, and being positive is a must. At least sixty girls turn out that first night. Some won't stay long enough to put their shorts and shoes on. They get psyched out by some flashy kid dribbling around the floor or they find out there are weekend practices (they weren't listening at the preseason meeting) and they depart immediately.

EVALUATING PERSONNEL SKILLS

Tryouts are the one part of the season where you are apt to make the most mistakes or the biggest mistakes. It is not unusual to have three or four times as many girls try out for your team as will actually make it. Your job is to evaluate all of the players and determine which you think will be the best group. You are not choosing individuals; you are choosing a team.

In looking at forty to fifty players, you can easily be tempted to look at the flashy moves of individuals. The quick dribbler will catch your eye, but you must evaluate her total skills. Can she pass, shoot, jump? Can she move laterally and backward with speed and agility? Few coaches check backward movement during tryouts, which is surprising when you consider how much time a basketball player spends during a game running backwards on defense. The ability to recover on defense is a prime factor in winning games. To ignore the backwards movement during tryouts makes your job that much more difficult during the season.

Today zone defenses are dominant. To defeat them you need quick, accurate passes and good outside shooting. They all want to shoot and score even though they lack self-confidence, causing them to be apprehensive to shoot during a game. Shooters are easy to find. Good shooters under pressure and experiencing fatigue are a more rare breed. Save your shooting tests for the end of a tryout session after you have looked at speed, agility, reaction, flexibility, coordination, passing, and dribbling. In other words, get the players tired and put a tight defense on them when you judge their shooting.

Regrettably one of the most neglected areas of the game is the assist. To have an assist credited to your name, you must be an accurate passer and have the ability to see where your open teammates are. All players are taught to hold the ball in a triple threat position—both hands on the ball in front of the chest, enabling them to choose to dribble, pass, or shoot. The passer must be able to put the ball in that position. She must be able to do so consistently. Add to the accuracy, touch. If a pass is thrown too lightly, it can easily be picked off and taken the opposite direction and burn you for two quick ones. Conversely, a bullet will simply fly through the receiver's hands, again causing a turnover. Touch and accuracy are essential for a successful pass, and passes are essential for a winning team. It is the pass that sets up the basket as an assist or the overall play on the outlet. Test for passing under tight pressure and with much movement taking place.

Jumping ability can be improved over a season but only to a minor degree. Increased height achievement should be developed over the off-season. The super jumper will be evident immediately. What must be sought in tryouts is the average-ability jumping player who is knowledgeable in positioning and is willing to get into the thick of the lane area work where the rebounds most often occur. The intelligent, eager, aggressive board player wins games.

The quick, rabbit-like dribbler will often get the ball down court against any pressure defense but only if she can use both hands. Too many players are content to use only their dominant hand. The first two-hand test can be a lining up of cones and asking the players to weave through them down the court. Use players as defenders on a second run.

EVALUATING THE INTANGIBLES

Evaluating skills is relatively easy when juxtaposed to the difficult task of determining a player's basketball sense, attitude and playing desire. Many players spend long, lonely hours in the driveway dribbling around on the cement and taking shots at the hoop up on the garage. Those long hours will obviously improve skills, but they will not enhance the sense necessary to make an efficient, productive team player. Knowing when to attack, recognizing when an opening occurs, keeping court balance, determining when to set a pick are all a necessary part of the game. Some time during each tryout session must be given to scrimmage-like play to seek the floor sense of the players. This time can simply be two on two or three on three or modified drills that may resemble scrimmage or game conditions, but something other than straight skill drills are needed.

Scrimmage work will also tell you a great deal about the player's attitude. Is team work and team success whatever group she is placed with more important than individual showmanship? Is she willing to work with anyone or does she seem to be more interested in her group or clique? Does she acknowledge good play of others or does she tend to criticize other's errors? You are the coach and you make the corrections. Players must accept their role as players only. Negativism or criticism of teammates generates dissension among the other members of the team. Only encouragement can be given by players regardless of what occurs. The player must be willing to accept correction from the coach; she must be willing to try whatever is asked.

Finally a player's playing desire is often a determining factor in making the team. Don't just watch the players on the floor; watch those on the sideline who are waiting their turn to get into the drill or scrimmage. Are they attentive to what is said and done? Or are they too busy talking with others, not knowing what is going on? When you have to repeatedly explain a basic drill, you have to question a player's desire to actually play. Desire spells a good bit about the player. When called upon to participate, the player who steps forward immediately obviously wants to play. Those who hang back may be short on confidence but desire is also a factor. You want players who want to play the game any time—not just in an official game but anytime they are near a court or ball and bucket. They will stay in the thick of the game regardless of the score. While you as a coach can improve upon desire with motivational techniques, there must be a desire that can be increased.

CHOOSING BY POSITION

Eventually you are going to have to decide upon that final group who will be the team. Even after experience you may make mistakes. But there are ways of cutting down on those mistakes. I have found that choosing a team by position is a major reason for our team's success. Each school has its own program, deciding upon how many players the team will have. Our program has had twelve players on the varsity and twelve on the junior varsity.

In selecting my twelve, I look first for two centers. Facing reality is a must and regardless of the many tomes written about quick, agile players, you cannot win consistently unless you have adequate height. You don't need dominant height to win, but you must have some. Centers don't have to be the main ingredient in your offensive attack but for you to have some degree of control on the boards, even with great positioning and blocking out, you still need some height to have fair control of the backboard. Be realistic and look for people who serve in this capacity. From the centers, I move to the forward position.

In the forward role, I look for a variety of sizes and skills. There should be some height and good body size to work the boards. Conversely, you need the beanpole, quick forwards to work on the opponent's bulky forwards. One of the forwards you choose should also be of medium size to go at forward and guard. The season gets long, and injuries become a factor too many times. Versatility in your lineup becomes a key factor.

For guards, the key ingredient in the repertoire of skills must be ball handling and basketball sense. They are your first line of defense and they run your offense. It is imperative that they understand the game or have the native intelligence to learn it. In choosing the guards, you should again look for a player of medium size who can go both at guard and forward. Two of this kind of player gives you the depth you need without having a bench filled with extra bodies who seldom get an opportunity to play. Your dual capacity players provide the depth, and you can have happy players because they are getting playing time.

After evaluating physical skills and intangible aspects of each player trying out for the team, you will find a group of players tied in abilities; that is, you aren't sure who the final twelve will be. You are sure of nine or ten, but there are at least two or three positions on the roster that four or five players could fill. You must ask yourself what is the biggest weakness as a group of those you have selected for the team. Then evaluate the individual strengths of those who are still vying for the team.

If you are lacking quickness, you may want to take a player for her quickness and make her a defensive specialist. If you have only average height, you may want to take the one six-footer trying out, even though she may lack ball handling skills or shooting touch. You can teach her rebounding techniques which are crucial for all teams.

And while physical skills are important, so are the emotional strengths of a team. If you don't have an emotional sparkplug, someone who can fire up the team, one of your open slots should be filled by such a player. She may not be a great player, but she has enough skill to contribute and she has an essential ingredient that every team needs. She may be the cheerleader type or a gifted comedienne, but she has the ability to emotionally awaken the team. She is vital in keeping your season from becoming a long, grim mechanical process. Only once did I choose a team without such a person and that mistake will never be made again.

Your selections, then, are made primarily by seeking specific skills for specific positions. It is when you come down to the last few spots on the roster that you must evaluate team weaknesses and when possible compensate for those weaknesses through your final selections. Remember you will need some height, some quickness, some speed, some shooting, some ball handling, and yes, some laughter. Rarely will one person bring all of these to a team. Your job is to choose those who as a group bring it all to a team and then blend it into a working unit. You're not going to get an All-Star team. You're going to get a group of varied skills and abilities; you put those together and with enough of the right work you can mold a team.

Once you have chosen the team, cease any thoughts about who else could have made it or maybe should have made it instead of someone who did. Once you post the list of players comprising your team, it is the *team*. Live with it, even if you made a mistake. If after a week or two, you realize that one of the players doesn't really have the potential you thought that she had, she is still a part of the team. Give her your attention just as you do the others. Hard work may provide the skill that natural talent hasn't. Remember you made the mistake, she didn't.

DETERMINING OFFENSES BY PEOPLE

The same night you make the final cut sit down and decide what offense you will begin with. Evaluate the team size and speed. Decide if you have enough height to work low post, or if it is a drought year for giants, you must go to a high post. My mid-post offense in Chapter 4 has been my answer to adequate but not dominant height. If you know the general makeup of your opponents, decide if they use a majority of zone or man-to-man defenses. Your initial team effort offensively must be aimed at the majority of what you will face. Once the season begins you prepare for each game individually, in a limited sense, but in those weeks when you are putting together a team before that first game, you must concentrate on building a basic framework that you can add to as the season progresses.

Don't let yourself get caught aiming for one strong rival or at a known tournament foe who has foiled your dreams in the past. A basketball season should be thought of as a stairway. Take it one step at a time; don't try skipping any and don't take a running leap to jump to the top step. You will only trip, hit your shins and painfully begin climbing again.

Further, don't make the mistake seen too often on teams. The coach played fast-break basketball in college and that's all she knows as offense. Her team is chosen and now she is going to teach her one offense. Maybe she knows others but that is her favorite. The fact that she doesn't have speed or height to run a fast break seems to be irrelevant to her. It's her favorite, it's what she knows, and lo and behold, that's what her team is going to use. The same holds true for the one-zone offense coach. This coach has been in the profession for four years now and from the opening year she has used this one offense. In her first year she had a good measure of success with it. What she hasn't realized is that with the players she had that year she could have used almost any offense and success would have been attained. Since the first year, success has been limited. The offense didn't match up with the players' abilities since then but she hasn't realized it. That is the essence of selecting an offense.

Look at the skills and potential ability of the people that you have chosen for the team and use an offense that takes advantage of those skills. Don't try to force something that isn't there. When you do, you create very frustrated players and a very frustrated coach who tends to start blaming lack of effort on the players' part because plans aren't working out as designed. Be realistic. If you don't have adequate height to control the boards you are not going to be a predominantly fast-breaking team. Have a little patience and use an offense that will incorporate the players' skills and talents. If you lack quickness and speed, find a good zone offense that relies on good passing. Passing can be taught much faster than speed can be developed.

The key to choosing a good offense is finding one that utilizes the skills of the players you have on the team and one that the players can learn. If you look at the practice schedule presented earlier you will see that little time is devoted to offense. With 20-30 minutes a day spent on offense, there is little point in selecting one that is complex with many cutters because you don't have the time to perfect the timing on which the plays depend and, further, you have no guarantee that the players will learn it at the same rate. A simpler offense can be learned by the majority of the players at the same rate. On the court, when you are teaching an offense, it is the same situation as when you are in the classroom teaching the conjugation of verbs or the functions of the digestive system. Not all of the players nor students learn at the same rate. In basketball, you want a majority of the players to be learning at the same time. Reduce your reteaching time by selecting an offense that can be learned mentally and can be accomplished physically.

3

FORMING YOUR OFFENSIVE
AND DEFENSIVE SHELLS
IN PRESEASON

EVERYONE LEARNS EVERYONE'S JOB

To make it through an entire basketball season with a high degree of success, you need players with endurance, good health, and knowledge. While you select a team on the basis of their skills for a particular position, it is imperative that each player learn all positions in terms of responsibilities. She must not only know where a player is on the court, but she must also know why she is there. To accomplish this objective, ask your players to buy a special notebook and after practices include in it all of the newly presented material from that day. Each offense, defense, and special situation play should be diagrammed and fully explained with each position receiving attention, not just her own. Periodically have the playbooks turned in for your perusal. Note errors and vague descriptions. Ask for addition of any play that is missing.

The use of playbooks prepared by the players will be of tremendous help to you in many ways. You find out who is listening, who really is interested in the game, not just in playing it. You find who is a team player. Those who can only describe their own role generally have one reason for not knowing the others; they're not interested. To make it through a season even though illness and injury hit, you must have knowledgeable people. One year, the same girl played guard, forward and center all within eight days. She knew all the positions because she was a team player, willing to learn the plays entirely and willing to play wherever she was needed. Her knowledge got her playing time while others remained on the bench, even though they were more talented.

To have a successful basketball team, you must draw upon all of the resources that you have. The greatest resource you have is the returning player. Not just her skill but her knowledge makes her an assistant coach. Because of the use of playbooks I was able one year to have a highly dedicated player who studied her plays present the mobile mid-post offense. I had planned to teach it to the group. I drew the lane area on the board, turned to the group, looked at one of my returning players and thought, "She should be able to do this. She played it all last year." Without any notice that would have allowed her to prepare a presentation, she got right up and taught the entire offensive set with all of the predesigned shot options to the team. She is not an A-student but rather one who works very hard at what she considers important. The playbook reinforced her understanding of the set; it was not a matter of memorizing but one of knowing. She remembered the entire offense over the long summer and fall. Playbooks work!

MULTIPURPOSE DRILLS PROVIDE PRODUCTIVITY

The short period that you have in preseason forces you to use multipurpose drills. They give you the opportunity to use your time as efficiently as possible with the highest productivity gained. Try to remember that teams are made in preseason, not players. You are not running a camp where individual skills are being taught. While you must use drills that will keep all skills polished to the highest degree possible depending on the individuals you have, it is team ability that you must capitalize on.

In the first few days of preseason practice, analyze team strengths and weaknesses in multipurpose drills. It is readily apparent if you have the talents for a fast-break offense. Without adequate rebounding height and speed, you must be realistic enough to recognize that you must use a patient zone offense.

A good test for determining if you can use a fast-break offense is the three-player weave, grapevine, snake—whatever you know it by. Run the three players both ways up and down the floor. That is, have the three weaving their way up the floor, ending with a three foot jump shot, rebounding, two people going to the outlet area with the rebounder initially taking the middle. There is no stop or hesitation and the same drill is run to the other end of the floor. Repeat the drill in exactly the same way, only add three defenders who know what is being done. Judge the rebounding ability. Is it taken with authority? Is it taken cleanly? Is the outlet pass made without hesitation? Are the outlets in position immediately? Is the flow of the play down the floor smooth or is it run too deliberately, which would cause a slowing down of the ball progression? If you feel you can successfully run a fast-break offense without spending hours and hours working on it, use it. Does it appear that some natural talents exist for the use of the fast break? If so, use it, but don't force it. Too many basketball teams have had mediocre seasons because the coach has forced upon the players an offense for which they really didn't have the necessary skill or ability. Give the situation an honest appraisal; if it isn't there be prepared to go with a nice patient set offense. A large portion of your practice time will be spent on drills and defense, particularly defense. It is the key to success.

Multiple defenses take time to develop, but they are easier to learn than offenses which depend so much on timing. With truly effective defenses you don't need a high percentage shooting team that is impossible to develop in a two or three week preseason period. The efficient, working defenses will give you the early season wins while your offense is still being developed that can earn your team a 16-2 record, as opposed to 10-8 because you spent too much time on offense in the early going.

Don't belabor the cause of the fast break in preseason. If you can develop it as the season progresses, fine. It will give you an additional weapon as you near tournament time. Multipurpose drills that will improve team weaknesses, however, are of the upmost importance in the first two weeks.

The drills I will describe are my favorites. Obviously all of us have certain drills we prefer. These drills are from other coaches, other books and my players who have brought them back from camps they have attended. The exact source of any of these drills is impossible for me to recall in that they have been learned and collected after many years of studying the game. My gratitude goes out to their originators.

Although this chapter follows that concerning tryouts, do not assume that everything contained herein must be taught, learned and used before the first game. It is not possible. As a matter of fact, it is inadvisable. All of these drills can be used in the preseason, but they don't have to be. Spend time on those that will improve your *major* weaknesses. You generally have two weeks to a month to prepare for your first game. Your role as a coach is to prepare a team for a season. That team is made up of individuals with varying skills, but the individuals must learn to function as a unit. That is your first, most important goal. The drills you use must be oriented towards improving individuals' skills but, more important, towards developing team play.

The Three-Player Weave

While many coaches use running laps as a means for conditioning, drills can fulfill the same purpose and improve skills. There are a number of drills that will include running and ball handling work. The most basic drill, often used in pregame warm-ups is the three-player weave, the drill you use to test if you have fast-break capability (Diagram 3-1). The

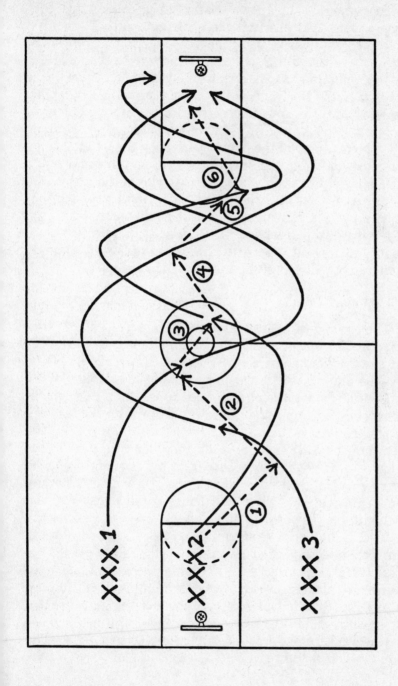

Diagram 3-1

players weave their way down the floor. While doing this, they are improving their passing and receiving ability. Three lines are formed as shown. With the ball starting at player 2's position, it is passed to 3, who is moving toward the middle of the floor going left. 2 moves right. Player 1 moves also to the right side of the floor and will receive a pass from 3. 3 then passes to 2, who is now moving toward the right side of the floor going left. As one of my players explained to a newcomer, "Just take the place of the person you threw the ball to." Move down court, finishing either with a short jump shot or a layup. In this one drill you can work on movement without the ball, passing, receiving, unit movement, shooting and conditioning. The players return up the side of the court, running, being certain to be ready for their next turn down the floor without holding up the drill. You can run it this single direction method or back and forth up the floor.

The Air-Bounce Combo

The air-bounce combo is also a multipurpose drill (Diagram 3-2). The players form three lines at one end of the floor with one line on each sideline and one in the middle of the floor. The players run a two-on-one with the middle playing defense. The sideline players use an air or bounce pass alternately. No dribbling or traveling is permitted. The offensive players are not to stop or come back from the ball. The purpose of the drill is to move up the floor with continuous motion, ending with a jump shot from the corner. Again, the players' receiving, passing, shooting skills, and conditioning are being improved. Further, the defensive player can work on anticipation of the pass. When an offensive player reaches the corner with the ball, she cannot pass to her teammate in the other corner because the defensive player who has played the middle of the floor must rush to contest the shot. This forces the offensive player to set herself but get the shot off quickly. It also forces the defender to practice recovery and fly at a shooter without fouling her.

One variation to the air-bounce combo is to allow the offense to add a limited dribble, three or four steps at the

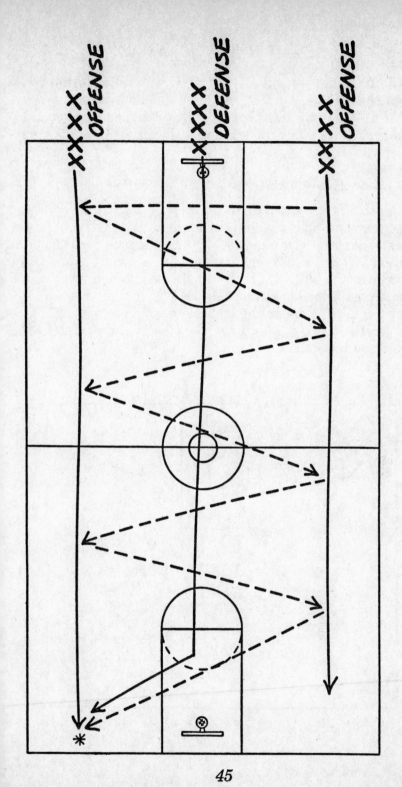

Diagram 3-2

maximum. This variation is primarily to aid the defender. When the dribble is added, the drill should end in a layup rather than a jump shot. The drill was designed for offensive emphasis. With the dribble added, the primary purpose is defensive work.

Four Corner Pass and Layup

A drill that can be used for skill improvement and pregame warm-up is the four corner drill (Diagram 3-3). The ball starts at X_1 who passes to X_2 and curls into a rebound position. X_2 passes to X_3 and curls into a rebound position. As X_3 receives the ball, X_4 breaks for the basket and receives a bounce pass from X_3. X_4 finishes the drill with a layup. X_3 is following in to complete the triangle rebound formation. The drill can be reversed to begin on the opposite side of the floor to work on left-hand layups.

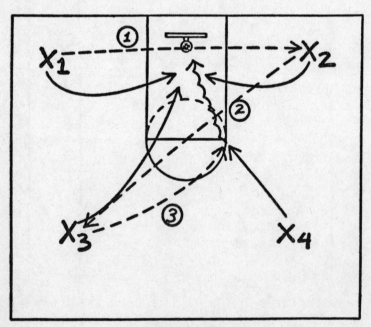

Diagram 3-3

Full Court Hustle

A tremendous drill for developing hustle and desire is a full court drill which develops reaction and one-on-one work (Diagram 3-4). The coach or manager stands at the free-throw line while the team is divided into two groups lined up on each side of the floor. Players are numbered in opposite directions. The coach or manager yells a number and throws the ball toward the center of the floor. The players with that number from each line move to gain possession of the ball. Each pass should be different, lob, bounce, chest, soft, hard, even rolled as a fumble would be. The player who gains control is the offense; the other becomes the defense, and they finish with a one-on-one with ten seconds to get off a shot. The variance of passes gives the players an opportunity to work on a more game-like situation. The rebounded shot or missed shot is returned to the coach or manager with a baseball pass. Don't forget to call the same number consecutively. It keeps all of the players alert, even those who think they have just completed their turn and assume they can now rest.

Change of Pace Dribbling

A good conditioning drill that also improves dribbling is the change of pace dribble. Three or four lines can be formed at one baseline. The players are told to watch the coach at the other baseline. The arms up signal means the players will be using a hard, fast dribble; arms down is a slow, controlled dribble. Upon reaching the coach, the players sprint back to the far end of the court to get back in line. Don't allow them to walk back. They should be hustling at all times. The practice attitude is carried into games. If you have walking in practice, you'll have walking in a game, and you'll never play .500 ball. Hustle is often the winning edge.

Change of Direction Dribbling

A variation is to work on change of direction with the dribble. The coach's arms are used as signals left or right. Don't use verbal signals. The players must watch the coach

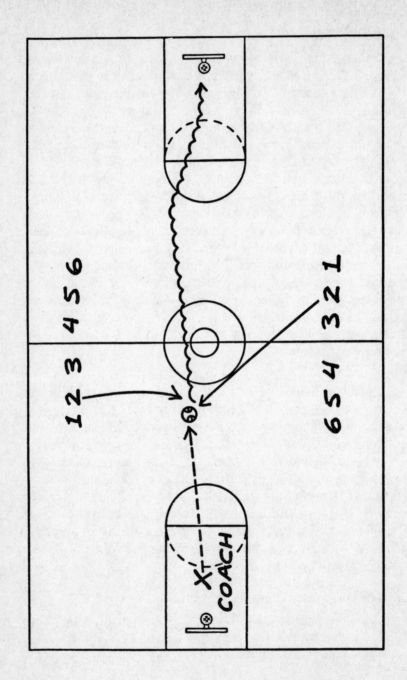

Diagram 3-4

and not the ball, which many will do if you allow them to. It's a bad habit all players should want to rid themselves of as quickly as possible if they have acquired it. It is preferable not to get it at all, but experience has shown that almost every young player comes in looking at the ball or the floor when dribbling. Even though you tell them that the ball is round and the floor is flat and both will stay that way, they continue with the bad habit unless you force them to break it. This change of direction drill, dependent upon looking at the direction-giver, provides the opportunity for them to break it.

Dribbling Through the Cone Maze

A game-condition drill that leads to many baskets is the zig-zag cone drill (Diagram 3-5). The drill is designed to have the players learn fluid motion on the dribble, moving their way down court, changing pace and direction as they progress towards the basket. The most important factor about the drill is that it forces the player to use both hands in dribbling.

Using the Multipurpose Drills for Pregame Warm-Ups

Some of the multipurpose drills can be used as pregame warm-ups. Pregame warm-ups are important to begin concentration for the game immediately ahead and to get the juices flowing. You want to get the team mentally and physically ready for play. Once a player is dressed in her uniform she does her stretching in the locker room. Each individual stretches according to her own needs. When the team takes the floor, it begins with the three-player weave because it includes so many skills.

Our teams have varied in their warm-ups other than the beginning three-player weave. Selection has depended on the personality and needs of the team. Some teams were slow starters so we used rapid movement drills such as the four corner pass and layup. Other teams were so effective in their full court zone pressure that we used a simple lead pass to a layup drill. Another team had a shortage of good shooters so they had spot shooting before the game; that is, certain places—spots—on the floor were designated and we formed

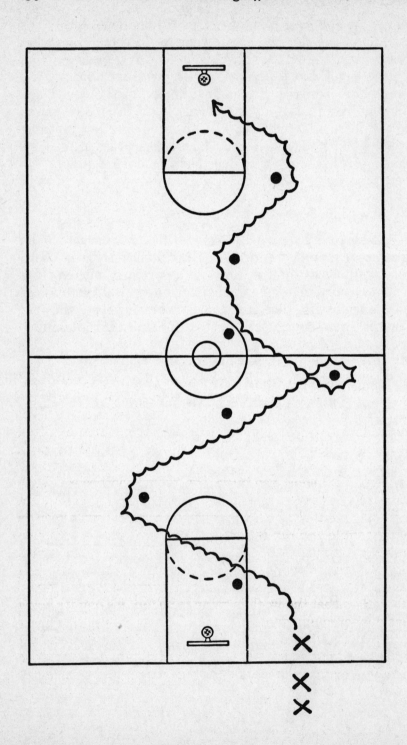

Diagram 3-5

lines where each player shot from those places, rotating to a rebound position. The pregame routine should utilize a variety of the multipurpose drills to allow each player to warm up all the required game skills.

BREAKING THE MONOTONY

The first few weeks of practice will fly by for you because there are so many skills and plays that you must work on and teach. However, you must put yourself in the role of a player. How many days could you, as a teenager or young adult with such a variety of interests, keep working at the same job? Practices can become boring. The second Monday you meet, aren't your players lethargic, almost indolent? They realize they have in front of them a full week of practice with no game to play—just more work. You will notice in the conditioners and warm-ups a spiritless effort. The players are going through the motions only. Ask them. To a player they will tell you that one of the reasons they came to basketball originally was to have fun. Running laps, rebounding lines, passing stars cease to be fun after a while especially when you know that's your menu for the week. The entire week strikes them as monotony even before they work up a sweat. They are more than a week away from a game, and they know it. That monotony will work against you unless you meet it head on.

You can spend the week appearing to be a cheerleader every day with short pep talks. I've known coaches who have done it, and I've seen coaches who haven't. It can work. I am personally not the cheerleader type in practice; I can't keep up a phony smile and rah-rah voice for a week. I find it takes too much time, time you should be using to work on the game. Your players are people and they have brains that work and feelings that can be touched. Don't give them a big con game, telling then that the week is going to be fun. It's not; it's going to be a lot of tough work. Take five or ten minutes on Monday to discuss the situation you are facing. The next five days are going to be long and tedious. The players have a tremendous amount of material to learn and skills to polish. By the end of the week, however, a team will be born! All will be working together for the benefit of the team. Each player will be responsible for the improvement of the group. Hard work is expected from all, enabling the team to be ready for that first game. Don't talk about a specific opponent until three days before the first game or you'll get them too high too early. Just refer to it as a game or the opponent. Keep the talk short. They've been sitting in classrooms all day listening to talkers. Enough of the words; get to the deeds.

In addition to your brief talk, make sure that you have a variety of drills to use in accomplishing the learning goals you have set. You can maintain mental sharpness by changing drills daily. Your players are not assembly line workers putting the same nut on the same bolt day after day. When you prepare your daily practice plan have five separate passing emphasis drills, five dribbling emphasis drills and five shooting emphasis drills; one to use each day of the week. By using multipurpose drills you can make minor changes to avoid getting into the same routine each day. The three-player weave, for example, can end with a jump shot one day, and a layup a few days later.

While you are working towards getting your individuals to play as a group, you must also have them thinking as a group. Each day as you shift from one part of your plan to the next, introduce another brief lesson on basketball that every player should know. It may come between defense and offense one day and between drills and defense the next. It too is a way of breaking the monotony, and it even provides for a "game" for your players.

While it may seem remote to you, learn to tie the "game" to their intuitive sense. It is curious and interesting to play possum, appearing not to be paying attention to them while they are taking a water break, but in fact be listening to every word spoken. What you hear are comments such as, "I'll bet we get our talk after defense today." "No, it was after defense yesterday." "It'll come after offense today and after drills tomorrow." These little exchanges tell me what players I will use in tight situations. They recognize patterns or try to interpret them. They are the thinkers on the floor. They hear the unstated, notice the unwritten. They are the players who can read offenses and defenses and can anticipate. Most of your players are on a similar skill level; how many are thinkers?

You may not be able to do much about their Economics or their French, but you can improve their basketball minds. Throughout the season, but particularly in these few early weeks when you are putting together a team before that first game, keep asking them questions. As you are working on your offensive plays, establish situations that will occur during a game. Overshift a defense and set up your players in a particular position on the floor. Ask them what they would do if they saw this specific defensive shift. What would they do if a zone was playing high on the floor, away from the basket? What would they do if a center was zagging in a 2-1-2 zone? What play would they run if they needed two points to win the game with fourteen seconds on the clock and all of the timeouts had been used? Do they choose a play you have introduced and worked on or do they try to concoct some remarkable gem right on the spot? Will the play they choose take four seconds or ten seconds to run? Are they prepared to work for the offensive board, because the second try at the shot generally wins it, not the first? These periods of questioning help their mental progress in the game but it also breaks the monotony of continuous physical work.

IMPROVING THE MENTAL ASPECT OF THE GAME

It is imperative that the players' analytical prowess be developed along with their physical skills. Game situations interspersed throughout a practice are a means of making them determine why plays are used when they are; defenses changed when they are. It is not enough to explain why you choose the plays and defensive alignments you use. It is necessary but not enough. If you provide all of the answers for them, they will not become thinkers, just doers. To make the simplest adjustment in a game you will have to call a timeout. Through a continuous effort by you in practice to challenge your players' thinking, forcing them to analyze a situation

they are facing, you will not have to waste timeouts. The
majority of them should be saved for the last few minutes of
the game, in case the game is close.

Finally, this questioning is telling you who is learning
the game. It is an oral exam in a sense. It makes the players
do something besides just move around the floor, following
your directions. Never be satisfied to have a player just a good
passer, dribbler, or shooter. Make her a thinker too. The
lethargy that exists during the second or third week of
preseason is a mental situation, not physical. The best way to
break it is to provide for a variety of mental situations that
force the player to do some thinking, some analyzing. Just as
physical skills can be learned and polished so can the mental
skills and it is the one area that most coaches ignore. They are
so bent on improving speed or jumping ability that they forget
the mental side of the game. If you have players that can make
their own adjustments on the floor, players that can read an
effort to break their full court presses allowing them to
anticipate passes, intercepting them and converting them to
points, you have a successful team, regardless of the final
score. You are contributing to the development of human
ability, a goal of the education process. Remember those
players are students first, athletes second. Everything you do
for them today can be used tomorrow—not only in classrooms,
practical everyday situations, but also on the basketball floor
when the team needs it. The mental aspect of the game is the
most forgotten and because it is forgotten you can have that
horrible condition before that first game called monotony.
Break it by physically and *mentally* challenging your players.

Furthermore, improving the mental aspect of the game
gradually allows for a shift of responsibility. It's totally yours
in the beginning of the season. You make the decisions. By the
end of the season, you should have an intelligent team that
needs direction but functions well on its own on the floor
because it has matured intellectually and can make good
decisions. Players should not have to be told by you, the coach,
every time the opponent switches to zone from man-to-man or
vice versa. The players should be able to recognize it just as

football players yell "draw" when a play appears to be a pass but is really a delayed run up the middle of the field. How much responsibility the players assume for calling plays depends upon their mental development. Their comments before, during and after a game will indicate how accurate their assessments are. Floor leaders must be trusted to have enough judgement to call an offense that is appropriate against a specific defense. Your point guard or floor leader should not have to look to the bench on every offensive trip down the floor. If you create that situation you are simply pulling the strings of your puppets and are inhibiting the mental growth of the players. Wrong decisions will be made but your corrections will reduce those errors, and you will develop a thinking team.

4

AGGRESSIVELY PLAYING ZONE OFFENSES

MEETING ANYTHING THROUGH SIMPLICITY

Every coach wants to have a team that grows and develops through the season. Each sets goals for the team to reach, and they generally include winning the conference title or reaching a particular level in the tournaments. From the opening day of practice those goals seem light years away. The most important goal you should set and one that can and should be attained by the first game is that the players perform as a team. To accomplish unity you must select offenses and defenses that your players can play. The secret is simplicity. Your players' mental abilities are as different as their physical abilities. There is a large group who are similar, but you are not teaching basketball to reach a median or have a bell-shaped curve. You have to reach all of them. This means you must limit the complexity of your attack and present a reasonable attack to stop your opponent. Keep both approaches simple but make them effective through repetition. Look at the truly successful teams in any sport. The consistently successful ones are those that have a fairly simple yet effective approach. The trick-play oriented teams occasionally make a splash but they don't make it to the top or stay at the top. Stay simple but stress execution.

KNOWING WHERE TO ATTACK ZONE DEFENSES

Before you present your offense to the team explain what a player is attempting to do with the ball. Score, yes, obviously, but while every defense stops various shots, they also all have weaknesses. It is the weakness that should be explained. All defenses have them.

All defenses cover specific areas of the floor, and they all have open areas. These are the attack areas, and your players should learn them. It is not enough just to recognize the defense; the players must know where to attack them. Diagrams 4-1 through 4-5 show the attack areas, the weaknesses of the noted zone defenses. Diagram 4-6 is the triangle-2 zone defense. Get the guards out of position by overloading them to one side of the floor. It leaves the other side open for short jump shots. Diagram 4-7 is the box and one. Some coaches still use this although its effectiveness is quite limited. Put your "star" for whom it is intended in one of the areas already covered by one of the box zone players, preferably one of the defenders on the free-throw line and overload the other side of the floor with three of your players. It results in two defenders covering three offensive players. (See pages 59–62.)

ATTACKING THE MAN-TO-MAN DEFENSE

Against a man-to-man defense the entire lane area and a fifteen foot perimeter become an attack area. Immediately attempt to drive to the basket with the use of a pick to determine the strength of the opponents' switches. If you are meeting a tight man-to-man defense, pull your offense to one side of the floor and send your best ball handler to the hoop. It comes down to one-on-one basketball. If you do not possess skillful drivers or an adequate amount of ball handling ability, only one driver can change the opponents' strategy and send them to a zone. Send your best driver up one side of

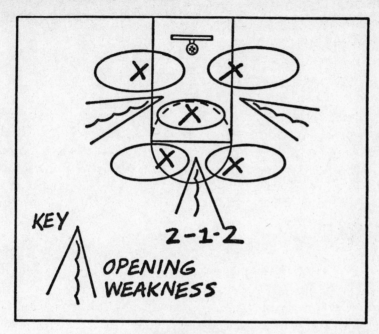

KEY

2-1-2

OPENING
WEAKNESS

Diagram 4-1

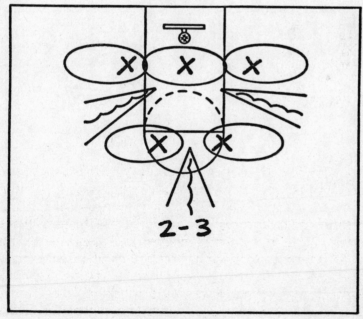

2-3

Diagram 4-2

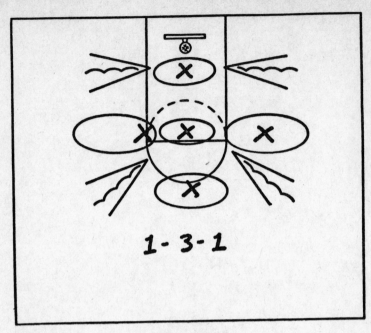

Diagram 4-3

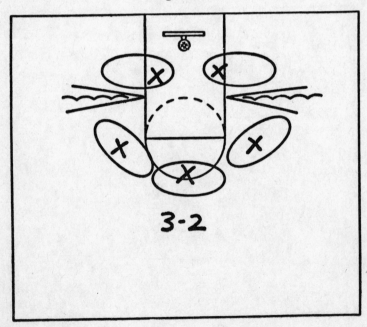

Diagram 4-4

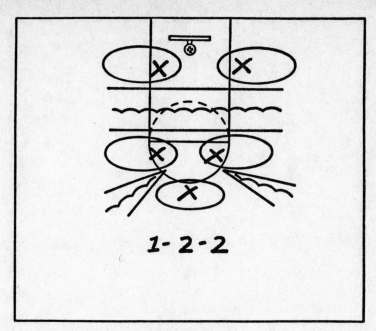

Diagram 4-5

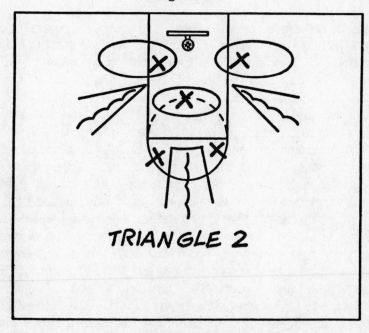

Diagram 4-6

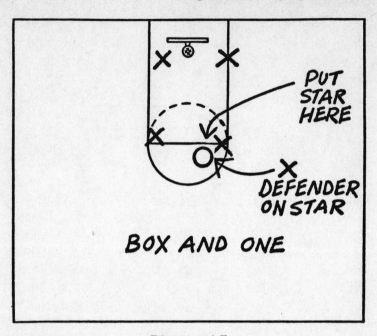

PUT STAR HERE

DEFENDER ON STAR

BOX AND ONE

Diagram 4-7

the floor for a move to the basket. Everyone else clears out for her. The next time down the floor, send her up the other side of the floor. If the defense realizes she is your offense, and it shouldn't take them too long, they will begin to sag off and help out the lone defender. Your driver should keep the ball as long as possible, drawing defenders to her and then pass off to your most mobile tall player, who goes to the basket.

It is important that each player have this information in her playbook. It teaches where the intelligent shots are against each defense. There is no need to keep gunning from twenty feet out trying to beat a zone if you know where to attack. If you have a consistent shooter from outside, fine, but ask yourself if you want to attack from outside. You may end up drawing your opponent from their zone into a man-to-man coverage. Do you want to play against man-to-man? If you attack a zone inside successfully, you will force your opponent to change to a different zone. Having learned all of the attack areas of zones, your players can move to different shot options of their offense. By causing your opponent to change from zone to man-to-man you may be getting something you can't handle as well. Girls' basketball is still developing and a vast majority still lack finely tuned ball handling and a knowledge of the game to play against man-to-man. If you can keep the opponent in various zones, your passing game remains intact.

STARTING WITH ONE MULTI-OPTION OFFENSE: THE MOBILE MID-POST

To meet various zone defenses you need a simple multi-shot option offensive set. The variety of zone offenses is innumerable because of the variations used in the basic defenses. In meeting a multiplicity of zones, my teams have gained the most success with my mobile mid-post. It presents several shots from all over the fifteen foot shot range and inside moving to the basket. The variety of shots allows you to use it against all of the zone defenses. Diagram 4-8 shows the basic set for the mobile mid-post. The center can set up on either side of the lane.

In beginning your attack with the mobile mid-post, the first pass goes into the center (Diagram 4-9). The center sets on the side of the lane where the ball is brought down. The ball should not be passed across the top of the key from guard to guard to get the ball to the side of the floor where the center is. The center should make her movement to the side of the floor that the ball is on. The cross-court pass at the top of the key is too conducive to being stolen. Against a 1-2-2, 2-1-2, 3-2 or 2-3 zone, the center can take a turn-around jump shot. Against a 1-3-1 zone the center will have to set higher on the lane and the jump shot is not open.

For a second shot option the center gives the ball back to the guard who has cut around to the outside. The center is in a position to screen and the guard takes a jump shot (Diagram 4-10).

For a third option, the center can pass to the forward who has moved outside away from the lane. The forward should be facing the basket when she receives the ball and is open to take a shot. The pass and shot must be done quickly; no time

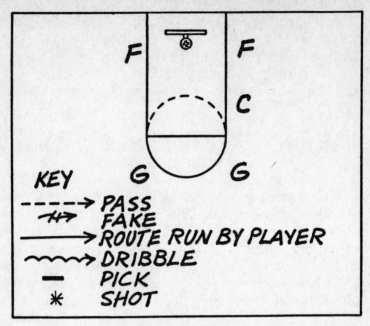

Diagram 4-8

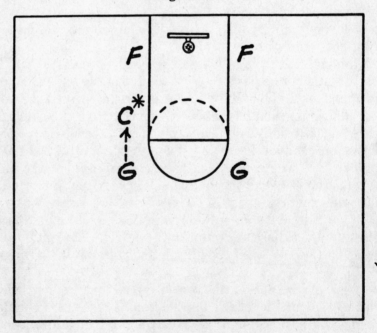

Diagram 4-9

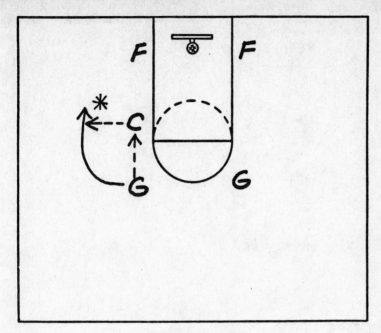

Diagram 4-10

is allowed for giving any thought to what is going to happen. A hesitation takes away the quick opening. (Diagram 4-11).

After the forward has established herself as a scoring threat from the corner, she has the fourth option in the offensive set to fake a jump shot and drive the baseline to the basket. Make the defender commit herself by coming out before the drive is attempted. It is important here for the forward to learn to make her move just as the defender arrives. The quick adjustment on defense is difficult and either an opening occurs or your forward will be fouled. (Diagram 4-12).

If the defender of the middle of the lane slides down to help out on the baseline drive, the center can now fake a pass to the forward in the corner and drive the ball to the inside of the lane (Diagram 4-13).

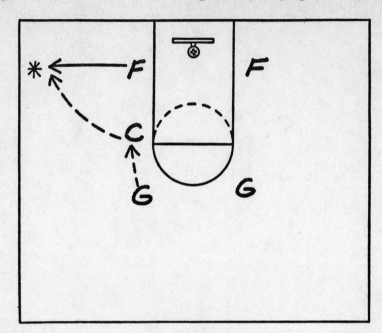

Diagram 4-11

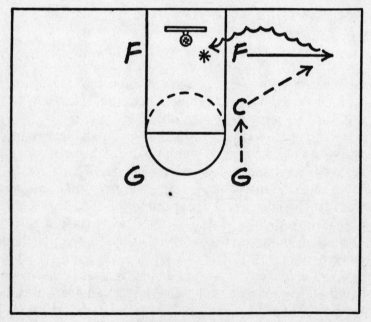

Diagram 4-12

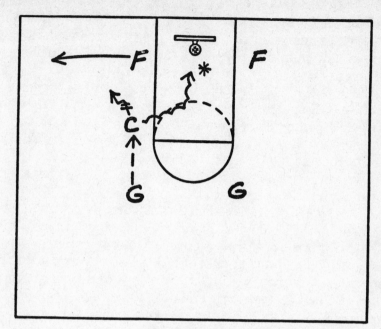

Diagram 4-13

TAKING ADVANTAGE OF THE DEFENSIVE REACTION

At this point having worked the same side of the floor, you have begun to draw the defenders towards that side of the floor. It will not take your opponent long to determine that the initial pass is going into the center. The defender covering the middle of the lane will start crowding your center, either planting herself right behind your center or risking fouls by reaching over her trying for a steal of the initial penetration pass. The defensive guard will either drop back trying to intercept the pass or force it in another direction. Those defensive reactions create other shot options.

The play-directing guard brings the ball down the floor nearer the sideline when she realizes the defensive people have been drawn to her side of the floor. This is the signal to your center to expect the ball to be passed more towards the sideline rather than into the lane area. Your center should take two or three steps out to receive it and look for the weakside guard who is cutting into the middle of the lane. The weakside guard will have a lay-up shot because the zone defense has been split in the middle as the strong side of your offense has thus far drawn the attention of the defenders (Diagram 4-14).

The option made available because of the groundwork laid in creating all of the early activity on one side of the floor is for the center in receiving the ball wide to pass to the weakside forward who is cutting into the lane after faking a step to the outside (Diagram 4-15).

With these two penetrating moves you have now established a direct weakside attack.

Once you have established that the first pass is going into the center, the defensive guards do not expect a pass from offensive guard to offensive guard. Generally they are sagging, trying to prevent the initial penetration pass to the center. You can now pass guard to guard and from guard to forward who has moved up and out to the ball. The forward can take a jump shot and drive in with a one-on-one move on the deep defender (Diagram 4-16).

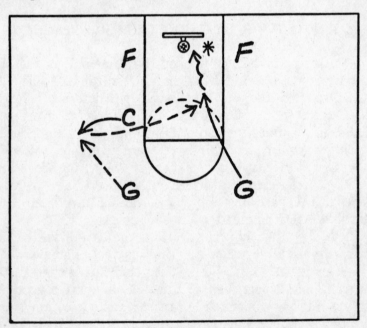

Diagram 4-14

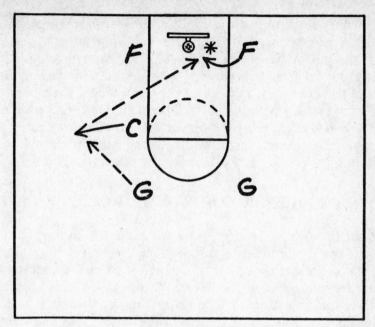

Diagram 4-15

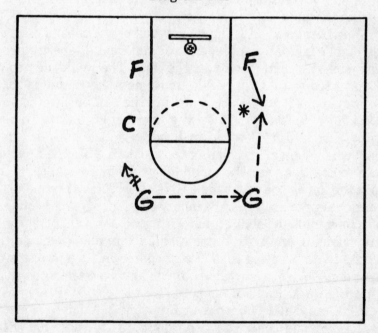

Diagram 4-16

The mobile mid-post is successful because you are always making a penetration move or establishing a pattern to do so. It is simple to learn and execute, and yet it is productive because it creates shot options from your center, working one side of the floor only. Put her on the other side of the floor and you have sixteen possible shots. The mobile mid-post does not rely on one player; every player on the floor becomes an offensive threat, and perhaps its strongest point is that you always have people in position for the offensive rebound.

TEACHING THE PHILOSOPHY OF THE MOBILE MID-POST

In teaching this offense to your team, it is imperative they learn the philosophy of it, not just the mechanics. They must understand that your initial attempts at the basket are made from one side of the floor to draw the defense, creating the weakside openings. The guard cutting up the middle is not a feasible option to begin the game with. You must first establish your game on the sides of the lane before you can move to the lane.

Further, because I emphasize defense, I consider this a resting offense. We don't spend a great deal of energy needlessly sending cutters all over the floor. The weakside people are expected to take a few fake movement steps and do some arm waving as if they were expecting the ball but that is only decoy work. As in any offense, they are taught to expect a pass at any time and not turn their heads from the ball, but they know when they are not going to receive the ball and should move to positions as rebounders or as defensive safety at the top of the key in the event the ball is intercepted. The majority of our energy is used in movement on defense, yet this offense gives us a multiple shot attack with good penetration against zone defenses, and with enough balance in our attack so the defense is not allowed to get comfortable in its effort to stop our shots. We are predictable only as much as we choose to be in setting up subsequent shots.

The only added option against one particular zone, a 1-3-1, is for the center to slide down to the baseline after passing to the forward in the corner. Here she acts as a screen or the ball can be passed into her if the defender commits too far out (Diagram 4-17). The forward shoots or passes into the center, who has a turn-around jumper or she can use the sliding big player move into the basket for a lay-in (page 72).

While I have repeatedly called for the first pass to go into the center, it is not imperative that this person be your center. If you have a center who is not a good ball handler, but you have a strong forward who is, and she has better than average height, she could fill the role. This position does require some height, which enables the girls to see where the openings are.

INTRODUCING AND GETTING FEEDBACK ON AN OFFENSE

In your practice schedule planning, provide several days to develop your set offense. It is impossible for all of the team to learn the entire offense in one meeting. The highest number of shot options you can present in one practice and hope to have the entire group grasp is three. While the more intelligent players will anticipate what else is available to them as shots from the set, you must impress them with the fact that they are working as a unit, and they must all learn at the same pace because of the important timing factor in offense.

Before moving on to the fourth, fifth, and sixth shot options, have your players draw the first three separately on the chalk board and explain what each player's role is. While the first option calls for the center to take a turn-around jump shot, it cannot be assumed her four teammates will stand and watch. The guard who fed her the pass must circle to the outside in anticipation of getting the ball back for a shot. The strong side forward must move towards the corner for the same reason. The weakside guard must take a few steps as if to penetrate the lane and then move back to the top of the key, acting as a defensive safety. The weakside forward must assume the shot will be missed, therefore, moving in for the defensive rebound. The only observers in basketball are sitting in the stands. That concept must be inculcated in every

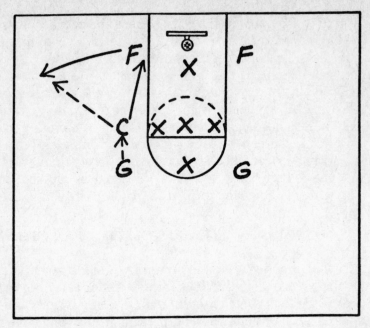

Diagram 4-17

player's mind. If any player chosen at random cannot fully diagram and explain the previous day's plays make sure that she knows it before you go on. Don't spend the rest of the practice session working on it but have a teammate explain it to her. Be certain you remind them to take ten minutes each night to update their playbooks with the day's new work.

Your players' feedback is vital to the team's learning and the executing of the offense. The only reason players resort to freelance play is because the predesigned offense is not working. The reason the predesigned offense is not working is because someone on the floor doesn't know the plays. The fault is yours, not the player's. Feedback of your presentation on a regular basis is a must. If you honestly want all of your team to learn the offense, if you want a total team where everyone has something to contribute, don't take the easy way out on feedback and continue to hand the chalk to your brightest player. Ask your slowest learner to do some explaining too. When she can teach the plays to the team as a reinforcement, you can feel comfortable they all have it.

PERFECTION GAINED THROUGH REPETITION

In the two or three week period that you have to assemble and produce a team before the first game, you can spend just a little less then five minutes on each offensive option each day. While five minutes may not seem like much time, in reality it is. To run option 1 of the mid-post offense takes 4.5 seconds, three seconds to bring the ball up the floor and 1.5 seconds to pass into the post who takes a turn-around jump shot. In looking at any one of the options, no more than ten seconds is consumed in getting off a shot. (You might want to keep that in mind if at the end of the game you have the ball with ten seconds remaining on the clock, tie score, you have possession and one timeout left. Use the timeout, check your shot chart quickly, see what has been most profitable for you and use that option. You will have enough time to get that high profitability shot off.) If you were practicing at absolute efficiency, you could take a total of thirty shots with the ten second allowance per option employed. Obviously this is not going to happen. You have corrections to make each time a shot is taken, directing players where they should be and where they should be moving to. As you begin the learning process of the offense, it takes longer to execute a shot option. However, in the second week of practice, the time required for corrections and refinement decreases and you will easily have twenty tries at the basket in the five minutes for working on that one option.

Working those five minute blocks per option is essential if the team is going to master a relatively simple offense. The key to point productivity in the early season is to repeat option practice. (Spending twenty minutes on offense and allowing the team to take any available shot as they are learning the offense only leads to confusion.) Tell the team you are going to work on option three. In the five minute block they know the shot is coming from the corner. You must watch each player separately, making certain each is in the right place at the right time. If the play is being worked from the right side of the floor, the left side—weakside—cannot be observers. The guard must make a jab step toward the middle, acting as if she will be cutting into the lane and then backing out to serve as the defensive safety. The weakside forward is responsible for the rebound. Seventy-five percent of all rebounds are on the opposite side of the floor from which the shot is taken. This forward, then, is the key rebounder on the third option. She must be made to know this. The right side forward must only be watched to make sure that her move to the outside is not made until the mid-post receives the first pass. The strong side guard who originated the play has the option of cutting up the lane or circling to the outside, taking a place in the shooting lane vs. a 2-1-2 zone. In practice she should alternate the pattern she will run. The center, after passing out to the corner, should think about rebound position and make her move as the shot goes up. The option should be run again, again, and again until all the players working together present a team effort to make the play work or until your time runs out for that option. The continued repetition of one option will gain far more favorable results than smorgasbord shooting. Only in the two to three practices just before the first game should you have your team run the offense, giving them the choice of any option they want. During this period you are looking for the sense to take the best shot that is open.

PLAYING THE SLOW-DOWN GAME

The worst actual bench coaching error I have made was in my first year. Our team had a four point lead with 2:14 left to play in the game. Our offense was not what you would call impressive that night. I called a timeout and sent the team back in with a specific play to run. It was the wrong move. I should have told them to just sit on the ball and make the other team come and get it. We missed the shot and our opponent scored. Another timeout was called. I did the same thing, sent them in with another play. We missed the shot, our opponent scored, and we ended up throwing the game away. It was our last game of the season. This error hasn't been repeated. One of the reasons is our use of the slow-down game when it's necessary. While many coaches claim they will never use the stall or freeze, I consider it another possible approach to gaining a victory. The stall does not say you are fearful of losing your lead and that you refuse to take chances any longer. What it really says to your opponent is that you have the lead and the ball, and that they must do something about it. And as for taking chances, in reality, the slow-down is a big gamble. To play it correctly, you need strong fundamentals in ball handling and alert, intelligent players. The longer you hold on to the ball, the greater the chance you have of losing it without even a try at the bucket. There are several slow-down games you can play, and Dean Smith's four corner is the most well known. However, I've used a couple of other approaches also.

The One-Player Stall

At the beginning of a season the easiest stall that you can use is the one I employed one year. We were blessed to have a highly talented dribbler who was cool under pressure. Knowing that, I did not spend any time in preseason working on a stall. When the need arose, I called a timeout, told the other four players to get themselves placed around the baseline and sidelines and told our super guard to put on the greatest one-player dribbling show the crowd has ever seen. If she got in any trouble, the other guard was to come to help her. In spite of the fact that three of the opposing players came up to defend her, she ran out the clock for us. If you have that talented a player, take advantage of it. If not, work on a stall.

The Triangle Stall

A triangle stall is particularly effective against a team that has been playing zones. (Diagram 4-18). When you come down the floor, set up in your triangle formation. You can run off 15-20 seconds just standing holding the ball while your opponent decides how to play you. Eventually they will send two guards out to the triangle and as the two defenders chase the ball, your three play catch. Soon a third joins the defend-

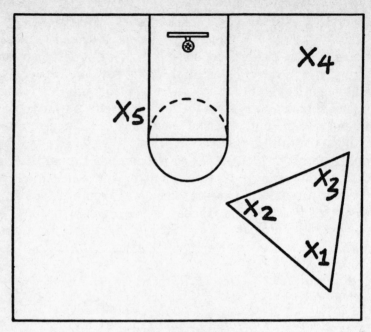

Diagram 4-18

ers to try to steal the ball or force you to move. If the three passers/dribblers have any real problems, the fourth offensive player, X_4, can move up and help in keeping possession.

To score off the triangle stall, it is necessary for the three players to execute their passing and dribbling act without the help of X_4. Whatever player is in the position of X_1—and it could be any one of the three because they should be moving—should be looking at the defenders of X_4 and X_5 whenever possible. If either defender moves forward to the ball, a pass should be made to the open player and she should drive to the basket. We keep moving the ball from one side of the floor to the other. Dribble it over, don't pass it. We want to test the defenders to see which is more apt to come out on the ball, leaving her player open. We also move the ball down to the corner occasionally just to entice the defender out.

Most players have little concept of actual playing time. In the stall game, thirty seconds seems like three minutes. Time with a stop watch in practice to show the players how long three minutes really is. To build that competitive edge on the team, divide the group into two teams. The group that stalls the longest should be rewarded in some way.

The Four-Corner Stall

The best-known slow-down game is the four-corner offense. We have employed it with good success and to the delight of the crowd one evening, and much to the chagrin of the crowd on another evening. It was particularly helpful one night when we were tired from having too many games in close succession. Our offense wasn't clicking that night. Because the girls were tired, they were taking too many shots from outside rather than trying to work the ball. We went to the four-corner stall in the third quarter and it gained us a victory. It was a drastic enough change to shake us out of our coma and forced the opponents into making many defensive errors.

In terms of running time off the clock, I look at this slow-down game not as four corners but as two sides of the floor (Diagram 4-19). Set up a player in each corner and put a good all-around player on the free-throw line. Teach it with the concept of two sides of the floor with a buffer zone in the middle. The player on the free-throw line can help either side. X_3 will slide to either side of the floor, not going deeper than the free-throw line extended. X_1 and X_2 are going to play catch. Neither should give up the ball until closely guarded. Make those defenders commit. When a pass from X_1 to X_2 is not possible, then X_3 comes to their aid; otherwise she should stay on the free-throw line. If your intention is to freeze the ball at the end of the game—i.e., take no shots, playing the clock not the opponent—you keep playing catch until you are fouled and continue to do so as long as you have the lead until the clock runs out of time.

If you are simply slowing the pace of the game and drawing a team out of a zone, then you must teach your players to look for openings and other open players. The weakside players can act as cutters along the baseline and X_3 is more involved in the ball handling (Diagram 4-20). X_1 and X_2 exchange passes. X_2 then passes to X_3 as X_1 moves to the

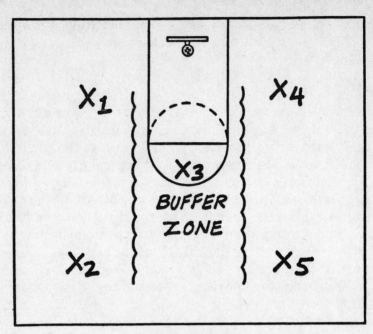

Diagram 4-19

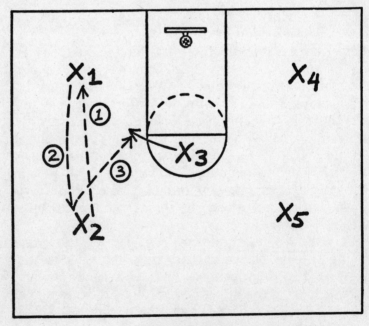

Diagram 4-20

basket. If her defender has moved from her zone defense area and has come out on the ball, X_3 passes to X_1 who goes in for the shot.

In Diagram 4-21, X_1 and X_2 again exchange passes with the third pass going to X_3. She pivots and passes to X_4 who has cut into the lane. A jump shot or layup is possible for X_4, depending on the defender's position. The ball should not be passed cross court to move the play. The risk of interception is too great. Let X_3 be your exchange player. Work both sides of the floor, again to see what defenders are most easily coaxed into the wrong position. With girls you can't use the long cross court passes that boys use. Most of them don't have the arm or upper body strength to sustain the normal four-corner attack. Hence, using the sides of the floor with the X_3 intermediary, you can still capitalize on the open weakside players.

The essence of a four-corner offense is patience. There is no need to rush any pass or shot because you have the lead and you are directing the pace. Anytime you are working on it, be sure you are timing the possession. Because you are watching

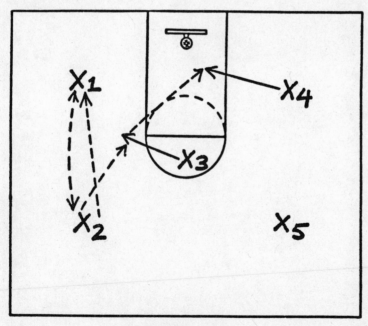

Diagram 4-21

the player movement, your manager can be your timer. In teaching it, stress working one side of the floor at a time and possession is the name of the game. It may have been a different game but what Vince Lombardi said holds true here too: as long as you have the ball, the other team can't score.

5

COACHING EFFECTIVE
MAN-TO-MAN OFFENSES

ONE-ON-ONE, TWO-ON-TWO TO MEET A MAN-TO-MAN DEFENSE

The zone offense or offenses you choose to implement will be used against zone defenses. You are essentially attacking the weaknesses of these zones or overloading one of the zone areas of responsibility. Against a man-to-man defense you must use a different attack. The zone offense will make your opponents' work too easy. With all but your defensive safety working towards the basket, your ball carrier is taking on four defenders. In playing against a man-to-man you want to take as many of those defenders away from the basket as possible. To accomplish this you will use one-on-one and two-on-two work to prepare your team for the man-to-man defense. Remember that in the early season simplicity is the name of the game. You want to be successful from the very beginning of the season, not when it is half over. While you could spend half the season developing a smoothly run cutting and screening machine, you are losing games in the meantime because your players aren't ready to use it.

As your season progresses you can develop a complex attack vs. the man-to-man. Set aside ten minutes of each practice to work on the offense for meeting the man-to-man and to prepare your team for tournaments. Your team should grow through the season; it should mature, but for those early games as a team it is still a child. It must be matured. You wouldn't teach geometry to a student who doesn't know how to add or subtract, would you? Then don't force a complex man-to-man cut and screen approach on your players until they have learned the basic man-to-man moves.

The one-on-one and two-on-two work can be accomplished in your period of drills. Every player on your team must learn ball handling skills well enough to be able to take the ball to the basket on her own. Obviously some are more adept at dribbling than are others, but each must learn enough to survive on the floor. Any time I've encountered the big player who can't dribble, I've instructed the team to play her very tight with hands high. As a television commentator so succinctly put it, "there are only three things that you can do with a basketball: pass, dribble, or shoot." If the big player can't dribble, she is drastically reduced as an offensive threat if she is more than five feet from the basket because when she gets the ball we smother her, stopping the shot or forcing a poor pass. When her mobility is reduced by ineffective dribbling, the rest of her game is also affected.

ONE-ON-ONE PRACTICE DRILLS

In our one-on-one work we make each player perform specific skills. Direct approach to the left side of the basket if she is right handed, and vice versa; a drive down the side of the floor with a turnaround cut to the middle of the lane, taking a jump shot from six feet out; and a timed possession are all required. For the timed possession, the offensive player starts at half court, dribbles hard to the free-throw circle and then makes the move she chooses. She cannot shoot before five seconds has elapsed, and she cannot keep the ball for longer than ten seconds before she shoots. This drill is particularly helpful in teaching a player that in man-to-man work you must not rush your play and yet if you take too long you give the defense a chance to sag in on you and have one of your teammates get caught on a three-second violation in the lane. It is also helpful in learning how to run the clock down at the end of a quarter, half, or game, making certain you get the last shot and that it will be a good shot, not just a desperation throwaway which is either too late or too early, giving your opponent one more try.

LEARNING TO USE SCREENS

Our two-on-two work in the beginning of the season is simple screen or give-and-go work. For the simple screen we have our people set up as if they were playing a zone offense (Diagram 5-1). We have G_1 with the ball dribbling towards G_2 who has moved over to the side of C. G_1 passes to G_2 who then uses C as her screen and drives up the middle of the lane. As she starts her drive the two F's move out towards the corner. C follows in a few steps behind. This can obviously be worked to either side of the floor.

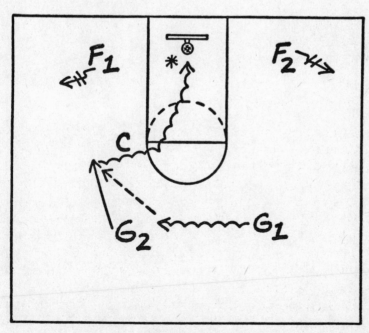

Diagram 5-1

The other screen we use is a guard for guard play (Diagram 5-2). We use the same offensive zone set. G_2 passes to G_1 and cuts to the middle of the lane line. G_1 dribbles around to the outside. F_2 moves out to the corner clearing the area. G_1 can drive in if there is an opening or take a jump shot at the point of the screen if a switch is made.

These are very simple screens but keep in mind that they are being used early in the season against a team who hasn't played defense together as a unit any longer than you have been together. They have not had enough time to refine all of their switches and much of what you are playing is one-on-one basketball. It is important in teaching the screens to have the ball handler at the point of the screen to cut as closely as possible to the screen to take advantage of it. It makes little sense to set a screen and then have the ball handler clear it by three feet. All you are doing is giving the defense room to break through it. Instruct your players to try to gently touch skin as they pass the screen. That makes it impossible for the

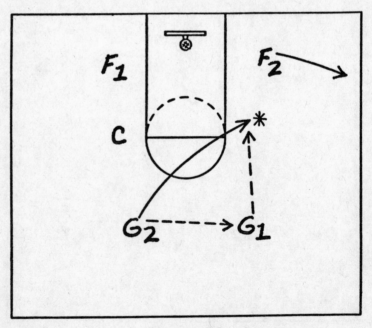

Diagram 5-2

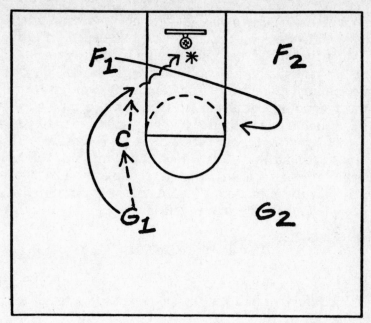

Diagram 5-3

defense to go through the screen; they must go around it or switch which gives you the split second opening you are seeking.

THE GIVE-AND-GO

Our give-and-go's are essentially guard oriented. Again we set in what appears to be a zone offense. The best argument for doing this is that it maintains floor balance, and it is not dramatically different from what the team has learned. Too many new plays in preseason produce nothing but confusion. Our give-and-go keeps going (Diagram 5-3). G_1 passes in to the C and cuts to the outside circling to the basket. She gets the pass back and drives to the basket as F_1 has cut through the lane and comes back for the rebound.

It is imperative that even though the shooters in most cases are the guards, the team should be instructed that

everyone has a role to play. G_2 does not stand and watch. She
moves to G_1's original spot making the opponent think she
may get the ball. F_1 has to be waving a very convincing hand,
causing her defender to think she will get the ball. F_2 jab steps
into the lane and comes out again. Each must give Academy
Award winning performances to make the play successful.
And each must be reminded the play isn't over until you get a
basket or your opponent gets the ball. No one shoots 100%. It
is those second and third shots that win games. First, the
players are actors then they are rebounders. Always assume
the shot will be missed. Be sure that you practice the give-
and-go from both sides of the floor.

ADDING FORWARD CUTBACKS

Our forwards get into the act in cutback moves (Diagram
5-4). Both forwards run the same patterned route but the play
will be run to the side of the floor where the ball is brought
down. The center must set to that side in what appears to be
our basic mid-post offense. Using her peripheral vision, she
will keep her eyes on G_1, appearing to be the primary receiver,
but she is actually waiting for the forwards to appear to her
side. When she sees them she fakes a step forward and then
cuts to the opposite side of the floor from the ball, clearing an
area alongside the free-throw lane for the forward to take as
she has moved to the outside of the floor, turned back several
steps to the basket, and then cut back to the vacated area. The
guard passes to the forward as she is cutting back. The
forward then has a turn-around jump shot.

The center uses the fake step to alert her defender that
she is about to make a move. If the center just takes off, her
defender may be sleeping and we have not vacated the area.
However, our ability to think and adjust without taking
timeouts comes into the picture again. If our guards notice
that the defense on the center is casual, they should pass to
her because the area around the goal is open, the forwards
having vacated the area to run their routes (Diagram 5-5).

If the forward's defender recognizes the cutback move,
she may cheat on defense and step in front of the forward to

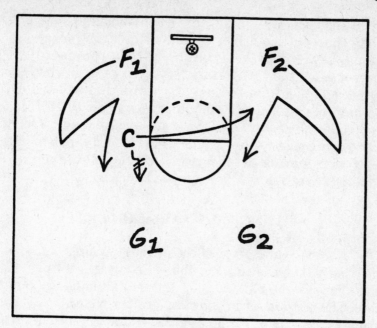

Diagram 5-4

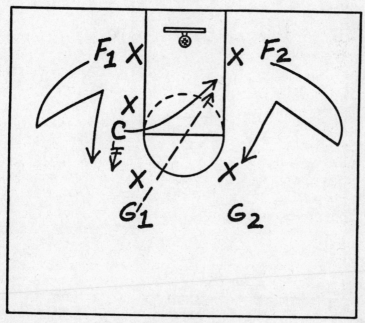

Diagram 5-5

steal the pass. It can happen once but should not occur more than that. On the defensive end of the floor your guard can simply say "lob" to the forward. The code word to move to the basket after the cutback alerts the forward to what is open because of the defensive act. In practice create this situation. In man-to-man defense you obviously stress the principle of protecting the basket, but you have a player cheat and cut in front of the receiver. Your guard and forward can then practice a lob pass moving to the basket for a layup. A few lob passes leading to layups will keep the defender honest.

APPLYING THE PENETRATION DRIBBLE

Another simple yet effective move against man-to-man defense is the penetration dribble. Regardless of which player has the ball, the play calls for a good ball handler (Diagram 5-6). The team is set in the standard perimeter set. G_1 uses a penetration dribble to the free-throw line. As she does this F_1

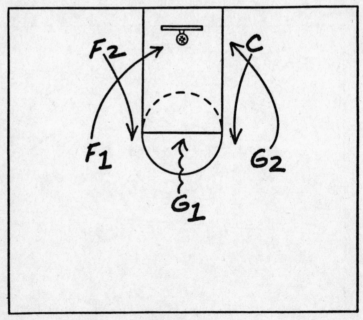

Diagram 5-6

and G_2 move toward the baseline and F_2 and C move to the ends of the free-throw line. G_1 looks for any of the players, one of the defenders may be picked off or be slow enough in reacting to allow one offensive player to be open. The play cannot be run when the ball is brought down the floor unless the opponent is playing full court man-to-man. If they are waiting for you and are picking you up as you come towards the basket, they will be too well established around the basket. The play must develop from various attempts to penetrate along either side of the lane. If the openings are not there, the ball should be brought out to the top of the key and then this attempt can be made.

FINDING THE OPPONENT'S WEAKEST PLAYER

A team of five outstanding man-to-man defenders is unusual. One is a little slower and can be lost for just that brief moment that enables your player to get open. The job of the team in the first few minutes of the game is to find that weakness. Therefore you must test every defender. There is a definite risk involved because you are not necessarily going to the openings which you will attack for the rest of the game or for however long you are faced with this defense. In those first minutes of the opening quarter, you are like a boxer in round one. You feel out your opponent, and you must keep your defenses up. You must yield five serious attempts at scoring as you look for the weaknesses. In so doing you are not going to be taking the highest percentage shots available. The boxer cautiously attempts some quick jabs. Can he get inside his opponent? A left hook is thrown to see what the opposing right hand does. If that opposing right hand comes up to block, does the left drop to maintain balance thereby creating an opening for a right cross? As you test your opponent, you look for what openings are created. Is there an eager defender who leaves her assignment to stay with the ball? Are switches called on picks or did you get a clear easy shot because of the bottleneck at the pick?

One of the most obvious attacks is against the opponent's offensive star. It is amazing how many coaches are willing to allow a girl to play only one end of the floor because she is an outstanding shooter. At the other end of the floor, she takes a rest. Not only can you score off her, but she will usually have a teammate who is defense oriented and will come to help out. When she leaves her match-up, you have another opening to attack. Both openings are caused by the lazy, ineffective defender. Remember that point and impress it upon your players. Offensively she gives up two possible shots. On defense, you give up two shots because of the lack of effort by one player who then gets the help of a teammate.

CONCENTRATING YOUR ATTACK ON ONLY ONE AREA OF THE FLOOR

While you have one half of the floor that is considered the offensive end, in reality, you do not score from the entire half; you score from one specific place on each attempt. Your players must be taught the difference in philosophy between using a half of the floor and attacking only one area.

In playing man-to-man offense you are attempting to gain one open spot somewhere near the basket where you can take a shot. It is obvious that you can shoot from mid court, even from thirty feet anytime you want. Who would waste their effort trying to stop a shot from thirty-five or forty feet? The percentage of success is so low that I would be inclined to encourage a shooter on the opposing team to try from that range. The full court presses are not designed to stop those shots. They are designed to inhibit dribblers and passes from ease in mobility. They attempt to create turnovers through mistakes in ball handling not howitzer attempts from mid court. Players know a forty-foot shot is unlikely to go in, yet they still try the twenty-five foot shot which isn't really that much better. In your man-to-man plays they must see that it is the fifteen foot or closer shot you are working for. And only one person shoots at a time so it is that person who takes the opening. When you are working for an opening, you must clear an area. You are matched up one-to-one so you must run a believable route that will take the defender with you. If four players clear to a twenty-five foot area from the basket, you are making it obvious who will take the shot and are encouraging the defenders to sag off their assignments to help out closer to the basket. Therefore when you are working on a two-on-two play, the remaining three teammates must stay out of the attack area, yet remain close enough to the action to be credible offensive threats.

For example, consider the forward cutbacks (Diagram 5-7). As F_1 cuts back to the ball, C must leave or there is no opening. G_1 can't stand and watch because her defender can sag back. G_1 must move to the outside, taking her defender with her. You want X_1 to the back of F_1 when F_1 takes the shot. The turn-around jumper will be taken to the inside of the lane. C must move all the way to the other side of the lane. She not only vacates the area but becomes the primary rebounder offensively. G_2 should fake to the side of the lane on her side of the floor and briefly step back. Because the play is run on both sides of the floor F_2's move is believable. When the shot is taken the players should be aligned as seen in Diagram 5-8. All players are in reasonable shooting distance and yet you have isolated your effort to one shot. Further, you have a defensive safety in G_2.

While a set offense against a zone has multi-options to run every time down the floor and those options are dictated by the kind of zone defense you are facing, playing against a man-to-man defense often presents nothing more than confusion even when your team is prepared for it. Because in most states organized basketball for girls and women has existed for less than a decade, the players' individual skills are not highly developed. Yet man-to-man play requires highly developed skills in ball handling. Most teams have one girl who will take on anybody but the majority shy away from it. Further, one-on-one play goes against the philosophy of many girls' athletic play. Most of the players are team-oriented to the point where they pass excessively, giving up openings. Their lack of self-confidence in their skills coupled with their aversion to being considered a ball-hog affects their

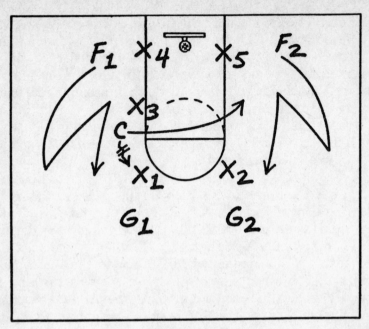

Diagram 5-7

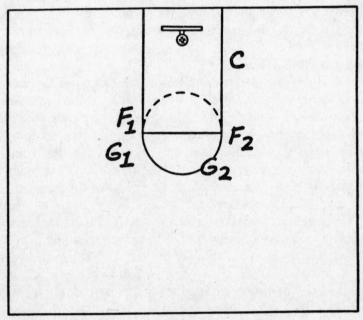

Diagram 5-8

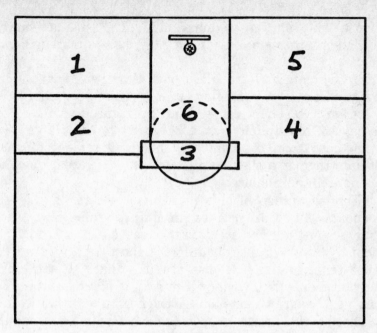

Diagram 5-9

man-to-man play. As a result you will often see one person take on the brunt of the offensive attack against a man-to-man defense.

To eliminate this problem (which it obviously becomes when your opponent realizes that one person will do most of the shooting), you must stress the team factor as a positive approach. Show your team how easy a game it becomes for your opponent when Suzie does all of the shooting. If you have a one-player offense, you don't have an offense. Each player must do her job if you are to have a team.

VARYING THE ATTACK AREAS *VS.* MAN-TO-MAN

The plan of attack must be varied to be successful. While you are attacking one area for the actual shot, the players must realize that there are many such areas. If a right side cutback works successfully the first few times you try it, you do not go to that same play five more consecutive times. The defense will sag into a makeshift zone, causing you the horrendous situation of trying to play man-to-man against a zone.

If the team has difficulties operating under this philosophy, you can divide the floor into areas and number them (Diagram 5-9). Then, rather than call timeouts to get your message of multiplicity of attack across to the players, you simply have to call out numbers. This numbering system does not limit them to a play but directs them to an area. How they get there is their choice.

The advantage of this numbering system is that the opponents will think you are running the same play. If you run a give-and-go from area 2 or if you set a pick in area 2, you obviously have two entirely different plays. Yet if you call "2" to the team and the defense assumes that the same play always comes with "2," it will provide a clear opening. For example, if you ran a give-and-go the first time "2" was called, the shot off the screen is open the second time because the defense is anticipating, incorrectly, the give-and-go.

A well-honed man-to-man attack takes hours and hours of practice, something you don't have. There are too many facets of the game to be learned in a short period of time called preseason. The team cannot learn everything by the first game, but it must learn enough to be competitive. A few simple one-on-one or two-on-two moves will keep you competitive.

6

USING MULTIPLE DEFENSES
AS AN OFFENSE

STRESSING THE IMPORTANCE OF DEFENSE

While every coach would like to have two or three sharpshooters with as many equally talented ball handlers to operate an impressive offense, the fact remains that we are fortunate when we have one. Most teams are made up of average players whose desire exceeds their skills. Their collective shooting from the field is between 25 and 30%. This means that for every time they take a shot only one of three or four will go in the basket. Unless you have dominant rebounders on the offensive boards, your opponent gets the ball the times you miss your shots. Without effective defensive play, it doesn't take a mathematical genius to figure out the results of a game where your opponent shoots only 5% points higher than you. To stop being out-shot and out-scored, you need a defensive punch—yes, punch.

Too often we think of our offense as our punch and settle for defense as a stopper. With the use of multiple defenses we add another offensive dimension to our game. Our purpose in defense should be to show the opponent many variations and to take the initiative on every trip down the floor, never allowing them to get comfortable in attempting to run their offense. Your defensive purpose is not simply to force them to take a bad shot or a low-percentage shot, but to preclude any shot. Every time you steal or intercept the ball or cause a turnover, you have given yourself another chance to get to your own basket and have denied your opponent a chance at hers. If your defense is executed properly, you will find that your attempts can double those of the opponents. You need to shoot only 10 of 40 while they are forced to shoot 10 of 20 to stay even with you. Defense gives you the opportunity to shoot 25% to their 50% just to stay even. With proper defensive technique you can win with desire, a quality your players have.

BASING A DEFENSE ON MAN-TO-MAN PRINCIPLES

Defensive technique begins with man-to-man principles. For your players to understand and execute overplay in zone defenses, forcing a team to go where its weaknesses are, they must first learn to play one's personal weaknesses. The many basic tenets of man-to-man are common: stay between the opponent and the ball when you are outside of the 21-foot basket area; stay between the basket and the opponent when you are inside the 21-foot basket area; overplay a right hander which forces her to her left; when encountering a screen, a player behind the action calls the switch; try to go on top of a screen if you are outside the 21-foot area, otherwise call the switch and pass denial which is discussed more fully later. Most often though, in an effort to make certain that these individual concepts are learned, the basic theory of defense is missed.

Consider what the game really is. One team beats another team if it scores more points. From the opposite point of view: one team loses if it does not score as many points as the other team. There is a difference. The first is an offensive viewpoint; the second is defensive. Further, consider the simplistic superficial nature of the game—a floor longer than it is wide with a basket at each end and a round ball to put in the basket. With that ball there are only three things you can do: pass, dribble or shoot. And that is the viewpoint that should be used when defense is taught.

DISSECTING THE FLOOR

In teaching defense have your players line the sideline of the floor and by placing yourself in various places on the floor describe and explain the very concept of ball awareness and the limits of the ball possessor. Your first job is to prevent your opponent from scoring. Being realistic, you know they are going to get off shots. It is your job to make sure they are not the shots your opponent wants. Do not work on the assumption that you will prevent only high percentage shots unless you know what their high percentage shots are. For example, if they have a "can't miss kid" from 22 feet, that is normally a low percentage shot but it isn't for them. You must stop that shot because it is the one she wants.

As you present the basic concepts of defense while walking around the floor, have your players always consider what options they as defenders must consider in relationship to the three things you can do with the ball. In Diagram 6-1, at A, the player will only pass or dribble; she will not shoot, so the defender is not concerned with giving up a basket. She can take chances on a steal because she has four teammates behind her. If she plays too closely to the ball holder, A can dribble past her too easily. If a rebound has just been taken and A is the outlet receiver, then the defender should overplay to the middle, forcing A towards the sidelines. Any extra steps taken give the defenders more time to get to their defensive assignments.

If B in 6-1 has dribbled to her place on the floor and the defender has stayed with her using the slide steps, she may pick up her dribble for one of two reasons. She may be right handed and had to bring the ball up the floor with her left hand to protect her possession. Unless she is highly skilled with the nondominant hand, her confidence will fade as she nears traffic. A teammate may have to come over to help her get the ball up the floor. If she's been dribbling, there may be

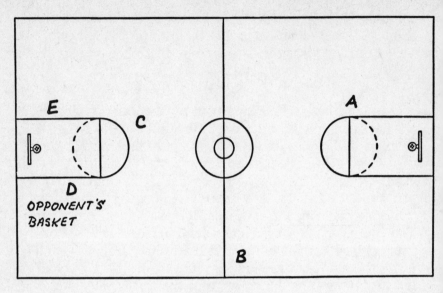

Diagram 6-1

concern for the 10-second line. As soon as she picks up her
dribble, she should be challenged closely by the defender. She
can no longer dribble by you, and she is not going to shoot
from there. She must pass; that is the only option the offense
has remaining, and that pass should not be allowed to be made
freely. The defender should keep one hand close to the ball
and one hand high. This makes the hip pass more difficult and
may cause a lob, which is easily intercepted.

If C in 6-1 has just received the ball, she has all three ball
options open to her. In the early part of the game, allow her to
take the shot. She must establish herself as an offensive
threat. Overplay her to the middle, giving her an invitation to
move to the outside. You do not want her to dribble or pass
easily to the middle of the lane. There are too many high
percentage shots there.

If D in 6-1 has just received the ball, she too has all of her
options with the ball. However, an immediate shot must be
considered and stopped. Considering her location, you must be

tight on her. You aren't going to force her outside with a dribble. D may want to dribble to the top of the key. If she moves in that direction, the defender should be prepared for a screen. That is where the majority of them occur.

If E in 6-1 has just received the ball, all three opportunities are open but a shot is of greatest concern. Because of her closeness to the basket, it is a high percentage shot. Many big players like to take that one dribble to get their desired position on the floor. The defender should look for this early in the contest. Does she always put the ball on the floor before going to the basket? The defender should plant a strong, wide base, forcing E to take one or two more dribbles than she would like to take. If she does, the defender's teammates will have time to sag in and help. E must be played very closely, prohibiting any easy move. The closer the ball handler is to the basket, the closer the defender must play her. There is no room for chance taking as there is in the back court.

DENIAL

When teaching principles of man-to-man defense, you must explain the concept of pass denial. Overplaying a player's strength, forcing her to go to her weakness, can be used on a dribbler. However, overplay can also be used on players without the ball. Having your outside foot (that nearest the ball) and putting your arm (nearest the ball) in front of the player you are guarding, discourages the player with the ball from passing to the player you are guarding. This is denial.

Your defensive player plays near her opponent and toward the ball. If she is guarding a player near the basket, she will "front" her opponent. It is especially important to deny the pass when the ball handler has used up her dribble. If all of the four defenders can play in the denial position, she has no choice but to shoot or be caught in a held ball situation. Players should remember that there are only three things that can be done with the ball. If the ball handler has used her dribble and all defenders are denying a pass, she has no choice but to shoot or be closely guarded for five seconds, causing a jump ball. If the defense has kept the ball outside on the perimeter, all that is left for the offense is a low percentage, howitzer shot from a low percentage area—exactly what *you* wanted.

TWO-ON-TWO, THREE-ON-THREE DEFENSE

In building your team into a working man-to-man defensive unit, gradually attain your five player unit. To do this, start with two-on-two drills using the full court. By using this approach you can inculcate the basic tenets of the defense as you explained it with the team watching from the sidelines.

Have two players bring the ball up the floor together with the defenders attempting to force the ball to the outside and denying passes. If you keep possession limited to one player, you gain time for your teammates to pick up their assignments. It takes far longer to dribble the ball up the floor than it does to pass it. All back court players should learn the overplay principle to the middle, forcing the dribbler to the sideline.

As the two players near the offensive goal, the defenders must begin looking for a pick and the pick and roll. Allow no switches in the beginning of play. Force each defender to stay with her player, using slide steps, not crossover steps, to get around the pick. If the offensive player is on the side of the lane, using a pick, the defender should slide behind the pick and move to a place on the floor that is in a direct line between the basket and the ball handler (Diagram 6-2). Because X_2 has a shorter route, she can beat O_2 to the basket.

If the offensive person is near the top of the key, X_2 should slide around the top of the pick and move to the basket (Diagram 6-3).

In both of these situations, a switch called out would cover the play better, but you should teach it without switches for two reasons. The defender must be aware of how much concentration, alertness and desire is required to play de-

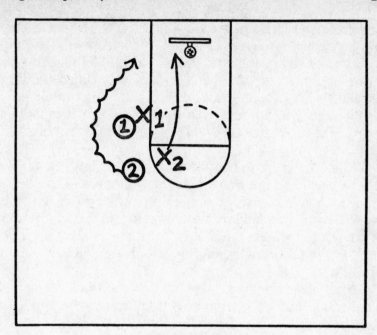

Diagram 6-2

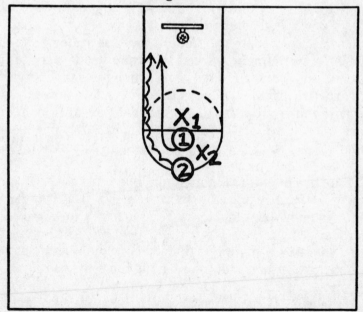

Diagram 6-3

fense. Further, when you are working on defense, you can also show the offensive players their two-on-two moves with picks.

If you have an assistant coach, she can be teaching the offense while you are teaching the defense. Don't allow the situation to become confused, however. If your practice plan calls for twenty minutes of man-to-man defense, it must have priority. The offensive work is frosting. First you must bake the cake.

When you progress to three-on-three work, be certain you have added a big or post person. Centers are key players in man-to-man defense, and their responsibilities must be clear-cut from the beginning. They do not harass quickly moving guards in the backcourt. It is obviously one of the more pointless ways of picking up a foul with zero results for their efforts.

Think about the skills the tall players have. They reach for rebounds until you convince them they must jump. A seventeen-year-old girl has had her height longer than a seventeen-year-old boy has in most cases. At thirteen she was already 5'8" and by fourteen 5'10". At that age the boys were still 5'6" and 5'7". Their growth spurt comes later. At that age she played basketball and found she was taller than her teammates. She simply reached over their heads, kept taking shots and came out the high scorer many times. She rarely has learned to dribble the ball, other than a few moves around the basket, if even those. This is what you are defending. Before we go any further, if you encounter the big, mobile, ball-handling center, put your quickest forward on her unless you have a center to match.

Your three-on-three work should be concentrated on the role of the center. Work on denying the easy pass into her by having your center play tight behind her, and a guard or forward sagging off her own player, stepping back toward the center. This will give away a jump shot from outside but that is a lower percentage shot than having the center bank one in from three or four feet (Diagram 6-4).

If the offensive center sets up outside, make her establish herself as an offensive threat before rushing out to cover her. If

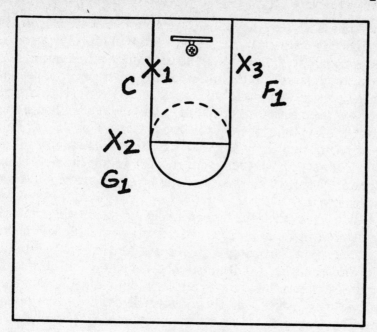

Diagram 6-4

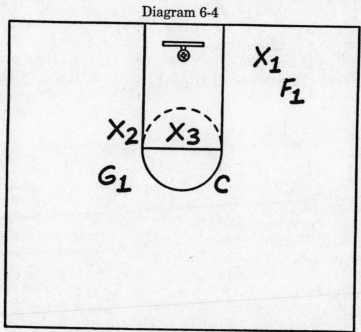

Diagram 6-5

she can't shoot from 20 feet, you gain a defender inside because you can sag off her (Diagram 6-5). Our greatest success against a man-to-man defense has been in pulling our center outside and to the far side of the floor from where we run a give-and-go with our quick guards. We consistently have seen the defense go with her, yet she never shoots from there; that is, she never establishes herself as an offensive threat. Our guards repeatedly have a one-on-one situation with another guard. If the opponents had kept the defensive center in, bottling up the lane, our give-and-gos would never have worked.

When we reach the five-on-five play, we simply state that player X, Y or Z has established herself as an offensive threat and then play accordingly. In a game and in your practices, you want similar conditions; that is, game conditions. Do something more than just a collection of neat drills; you don't always know what your opponents will do. For tournaments you often get one or no look at your opponent. You must be ready for anything. And you must be ready with thinking players. You surely don't want to use all of your timeouts in the first quarter telling your team what's happening. By using the limited number of players in building toward unit play, you can isolate the problems that can occur during a game.

CALLING SWITCHES

Once you have reached the point where you are playing five-on-five, you can teach the principle of switching, that is changing defensive assignments. Switches are necessitated when a defender is blocked from the path she must follow to stay with her opponent. This situation is created when an offensive teammate sets a pick or screen—that is, establishes herself in a position that is in the path the defender is following. The defender, if far enough from the basket, can move around the pick or screen and once again be in close enough proximity to the offensive player.

Because the defender is concentrating on her assignment she cannot see the pick soon enough to react properly. Therefore it is the responsibility of one of her teammates to call it to her attention. Again if the defender about to be picked off is far enough from the basket, 15-20 feet, her teammate simply has to call "pick" or "screen." The adjustment can be made in time to prevent an easy, quick basket. However in the 15 foot or less range, switches in defensive assignments should be made.

In making a switch, it should be the responsibility of the player closest to the basket who is involved in the play. Because she is deeper toward the basket, she can see the play better (Diagram 6-6). X_1 can see what is developing and should call the switch. X_1 will pick up O_2 and O_1 becomes the assignment of X_2. X_4 has the best view of the play but you don't want her to completely leave O_4 because of the possible back door play. X_3 can slide down through the lane and X_4 can slide a few steps into the lane to cover both O_3 and O_4. X_2

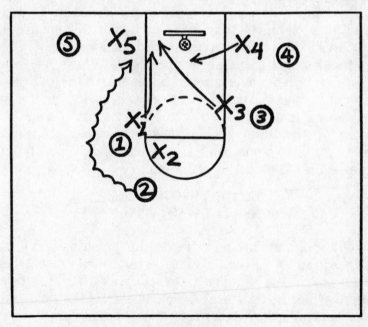

Diagram 6-6

should play denial on O_1 in an attempt to bottle up O_2 who has penetrated but is cut off from a shot if X_1 is playing good defense.

The primary job of defense is to prevent your opponent from scoring. These rapid adjustments will keep your opponent confused but you must be certain that they don't confuse the defense too. Codes for offenses and defenses are useful for team communication, but when you are calling switches, keep it basic. If Sue is telling Mary they are going to switch, simply have Sue say, "Mary, switch." There is little point in having three remaining teammates in doubt as to whether they are involved in the switch.

MISMATCHES

If the switch results in an obvious mismatch, which is what your opponent may be trying to accomplish, the team should not panic and have everyone sagging in to help out. It is likely that a center will be defending a guard or forward, a smaller player, and one of your guards will be defending someone much bigger than herself. Further this mismatch of body sizes will probably occur around the lane area. The key is to follow the ball and protect the basket. Don't rush out to help the smaller player unless that is where the ball is and then only when the defender asks for help. If everyone who sees the mismatch sags off, you have too many unguarded players who are in prime locations for easy baskets. Basketball is a team game, and the team concept can only be achieved if each player does her job.

FALLING INTO A ZONE
AGAINST THE HIGH POST WEAVE

One popular method of creating openings and mismatches around the lane against a man-to-man defense is to set the center as a high post in top of the key. The guards and forwards then run patterns from one side of the floor to the other, weaving back and forth feeding the ball into the center who passes it back out. The center becomes the natural pick (Diagram 6-7). By weaving all of the offensive people past the center, the offense draws the defenders away from the basket if they are playing a true man-to-man; eventually one of them is picked off without a switch being made or a mismatch occurs if the switch is made. The offense then takes the ball to the hoop.

The reason the defense breaks down against the weave is because one failure in communication allows the pick to be a success. Your defenders are playing laterally on the floor and who actually calls the switch becomes a debatable question. To avoid the question and the confusion created by a high post weave, your floor leader, the voice on the floor who calls defensive changes or special plays should call "weave" or "lateral." That one word tells your players to leave the man-to-man defense and fall into a 2-1-2 zone. The cutting, weaving pattern becomes pointless as your players protect the side and middle of the lane.

Your guards, the front two, should overplay the center, making it difficult to pass to her. Your center should be two steps behind the high post, ready to block a shot. Your

Diagram 6-7

forwards set up along each side of the lane and stay there. If the opponents continue to weave, be patient and stay in your zone. All you will give up are outside jump shots, lower percentage shots as indicated in the open boxes (Diagram 6-8).

You have your natural triangle rebound force ready while your opponents have no one in a rebounding position. They will have to be sharpshooters to beat you with this alignment. They will soon realize that the weave cannot be used against you, thereby showing them that you are deciding what they will do. If they continue to use the weave they will at best only get one shot each time down the floor.

It must always be remembered that all defenses give up something. Because of all of the movement inherent with man-to-man defense, it is a foul conducive defense. Unless you have a great amount of depth you can go to on your bench, you must also teach your players zone defenses. Their strengths and weaknesses are discussed next.

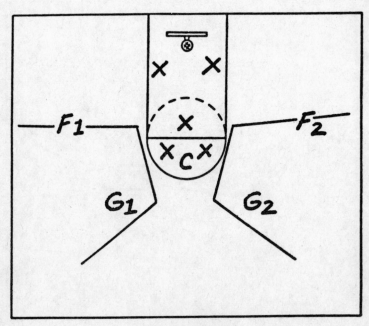

Diagram 6-8

7

STOPPING SET OFFENSES
WITH ZONE DEFENSES

Most of the offenses you see are a series of plays run from the same established placements of players on the floor. Generally the guards bring the ball up the floor with their three teammates waiting for them around the perimeter of the free-throw lane.

In recent years terminology has changed from center and forward to post and wing, but regardless of what they are called, there is usually a big player somewhere near the basket. The three-second-in-the-lane rule precludes that person from setting up in the middle of the lane as players did twenty-five years ago, so now they are close to the lane line. Two old standbys for beginning an offense are the low post (Diagram 7-1) and the double low post (Diagram 7-2). To counteract these zone offenses, there are a group of zone defenses. A third set offense, the high post (Diagram 7-3) can be met with the 1-3-1 zone defense.

Zone defenses are particularly effective because they cover a large area of the floor without subjecting your players to a host of fouling situations. While man-to-man defense emphasizes an awareness of your particular assignment, zone defenses are concerned with the location of the ball. As a player, you must always know where the ball is. You are

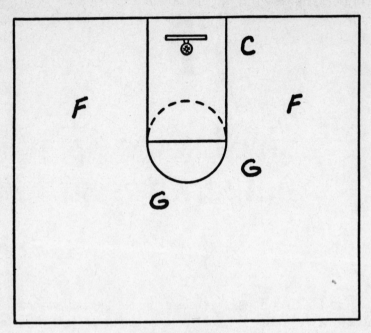

Diagram 7-1

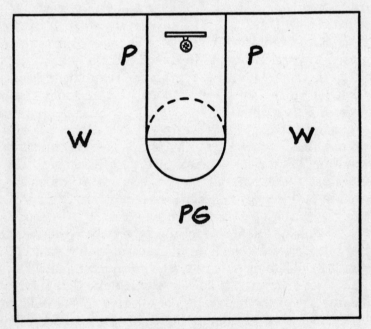

Diagram 7-2

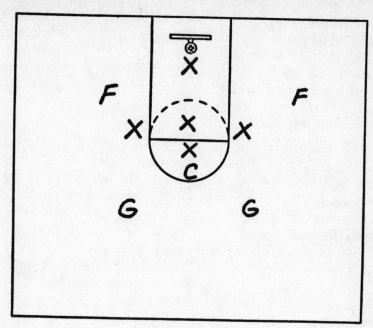

Diagram 7-3

contending with offensive threat, not the one or two players who are in your area of responsibility. Those players gain importance only when they have the ball.

MOVING TO THE ZONES

Before you can teach zone defenses and have them played effectively, you should teach man-to-man principles. For example, for your guard to play a dribbler effectively on the top of the zone, she should know the overplay principle to move the dribbler to the side of the floor, preventing her from penetrating the lane. By teaching basic man-to-man principles, you can play the zones from an attacking stance. That will allow you to act, not react, which leads to fouls.

In Chapter IV, zone defenses were outlined from an offensive viewpoint; that is, where the zones' vulnerabilities are, or the attack areas. In teaching defense, remember that all defenses give up something. What is given up depends on your players. They must always try to stop the high percentage shot, therefore in playing zones, you want to stop penetration into the lane by either a pass or the dribble. You give up the outside shot but only if your opponent is not hitting consistently from the outside.

2-1-2 Zone and 2-3 Zone

In teaching zones, you establish the area of responsibility of each player. In the 2-1-2 the most popular zone, the areas you are giving up for shots are those shaded (Diagram 7-4). A variation of the 2-1-2 is the 2-3 (Diagram 7-5). The center drops back, which does allow an opening in the middle of the lane. However, the center will move up to cover this area if a player enters. While a center plays a horizontal game in the 2-1-2, it more closely resembles vertical coverage in the 2-3. All players will slide to the edge of their areas depending on the ball location. If you have particularly quick guards, they can enlarge their area towards the given shooting lanes.

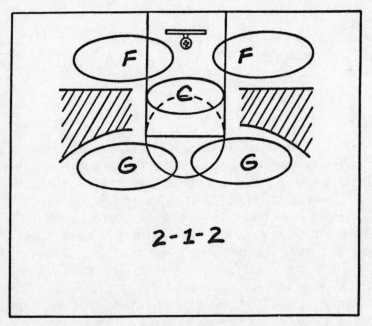

Diagram 7-4

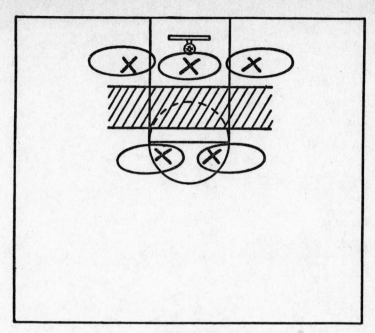

Diagram 7-5

If the offense is shooting successfully from the corners, the forward must leave her area to go out to defend against the shot. She does not leave until the opponent has established herself as a threat; there is no reason for the forward to run helter-skelter from the lane area to the corner every time the ball moves there if the opponent cannot shoot from there successfully.

When the forward does move out to the corner, the center and strong side guard must adjust their positions. The guard will move to the middle of the lane, stopping a direct pass into the lane because the center has moved down to the area F_2 has left as shown in Diagram 7-6. If the shot is not taken and the ball is passed back to the key area, all players shift to their original areas. Both the 2-1-2 and 2-3 provide good rebounding strength.

3-2 Zone and 1-2-2 Zone

Two odd man zones that are effective against teams that are lacking height are the 3-2 and the 1-2-2 (Diagrams 7-7

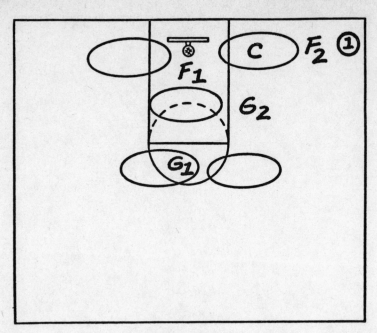

Diagram 7-6

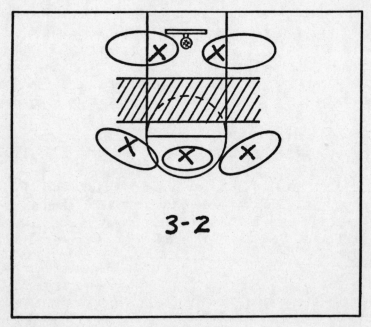

Diagram 7-7

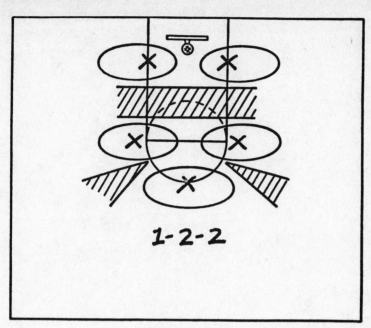

1-2-2

Diagram 7-8

and 7-8). The 3-2 and 1-2-2 both give up shots in the middle of the lane if your opponent uses cutters, but like all zones, they provide good rebounding strength. The 3-2 stops the perimeter jump shot, a weapon a team must have if it lacks height. The 1-2-2, often called the jug defense because of the player alignment with a neck, shoulders and base of a jug regardless of the ball location, is good for starting a fast break because you always have a point player to take the middle lane and two people who can quickly move to the outlet areas to initiate the break.

Box-and-One

A specialized zone is the box-and-one (Diagram 7-9), designed to stop one highly productive offensive star. Your best defensive player is assigned to cover the star regardless of where she goes on the floor while the rest of the team plays a four-man box. Give a lot of thought to your opponent as a team before using this defense. In reality, if a one-player team does

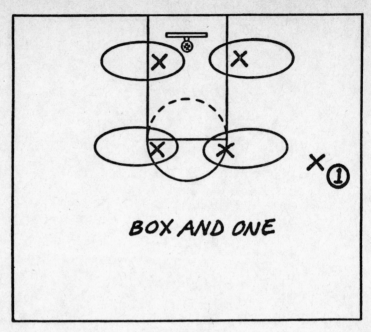

BOX AND ONE

Diagram 7-9

indeed depend on that one player only, it may be easier to give her thirty points and shut out the other four. If they are accustomed to relying on her for a majority of the offense, shutting out the rest of the team early in the game will force the opponent to depend on the star totally. Rare is the player who can defeat another team. Further, once you have established that dependence on just the one, change your defense in the third quarter, freeing the four but stopping the one. It forces your opponent to change her attack, and it may be too late for the entire team to adjust.

Triangle-Two Zone

Depending on your personnel and opponent, you may want to use a combination zone and man-to-man. The triangle-two (Diagram 7-10) is a good combination defense if you have quickness in your guards and your opponent's guards are weak ball handlers. The triangle-two should be a special

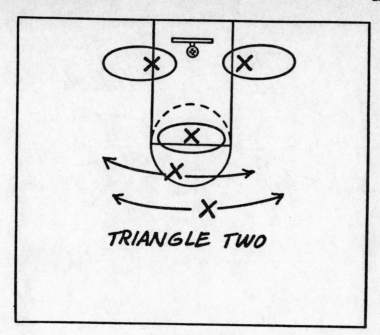

TRIANGLE TWO

Diagram 7-10

occasion defense and can be added only after the basic principles of man-to-man and zone defenses are learned.

1-3-1 Zone

The odd man defense that is most effective against a high post offense is the 1-3-1 (Diagram 7-11). Its greatest weakness is found on the baseline; however, that can be reduced by using a quick player, X_1, under the basket rather than a big player who may lack mobility. X_1 is better able to cover the outside because of her speed. As the ball moves out to the corner, X_1 must call for her teammate's help. For example, in Diagram 7-12, the ball has gone to the right corner. X_1 moves out to take the shooter and she calls out to X_2 to fall back and cover the basket underneath. She would not call X_3 because you want the lane protected. It is less likely a pass would be thrown from the right corner to the area vacated by X_2 than it would be for an offensive player to slip behind X_4 and receive a lob to the middle where she could take a quick jump shot. You can

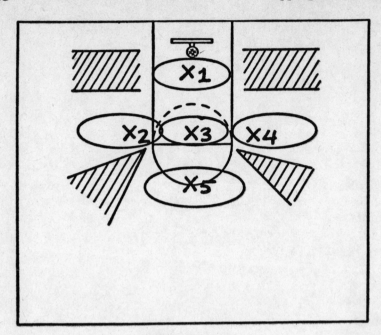

Diagram 7-11

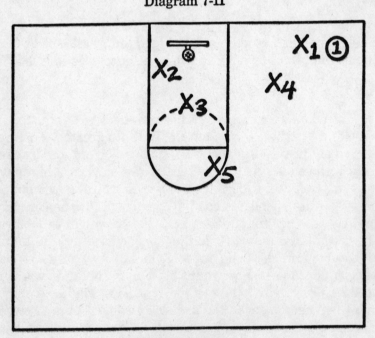

Diagram 7-12

protect the lane and the baseline by calling for the outside, weakside wing to move down.

If an offensive player moves behind X_1, X_4 should shift down to cover her and X_3 should step toward the side of the lane. By using a guard deep, you gain her quickness and the aid of your taller people, probably forwards, playing the wing, to protect the basket (Diagram 7-13). By stopping the shot or forcing one up from outside, you can shift back to your original alignment or have your height in rebounding positions.

In each of the zones you can protect your big player in the middle against fouls. While man-to-man defense forces movement of players, that movement creates many fouling situations. The zones force more movement of the ball, specifically in quick accurate passing and that decreases player movement, therefore reducing fouling situations.

These zones reflect only the coverage on one end of the floor. Zones can be extended to the entire floor and through their use, they can generate points, becoming an offense.

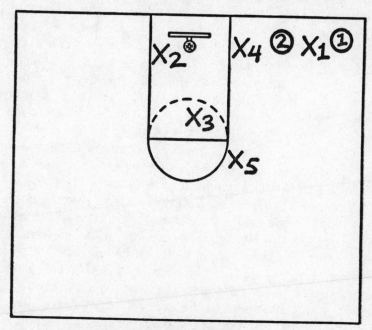

Diagram 7-13

ZONE PRESSES BECOME AN OFFENSE

Zone defenses protect only one end of the floor and in effect invite your opponent to gain confidence through the comfort of allowing them to run their plays as they have practiced them. Through the employment of zone presses you are telling your opponent that you will not allow them to be comfortable, that they will be playing under pressure, literally, throughout the game. They may successfully operate under that pressure in the beginning of the game if they have been taught how to deal with it and how to break the presses but eventually the pressure will build and turnovers will occur. If they have not worked on breaking presses, they will succumb immediately. By using presses you are setting the tone and pace of the game; you are dictating your opponent's moves.

2-2-1 Zone Press

One of the most popular zone presses is the 2-2-1 full court (Diagram 7-14). While coaches advocate the use of their taller players along the free-throw line, a strong case can be made for using guards who generally have better speed and can follow the ball handlers better, creating more traps. Further, from our alignment it is more logical to fall back into our zones once the press is broken. Also, I prefer having my center back protecting the basket. We see mostly guards taking the ball out-of-bounds against us and we prefer to match our guards against theirs, leaving the center back to defend against a center or forward who may receive a long court pass, creating a one-on-one situation. Set your alignment according to the personnel you have.

The three large V's in Diagram 7-14 represent the three main traps in the back court, the areas where you want the ball to go. Most of the traps set will be in trap A because a large majority of the time the ball is taken out on that side of the floor, most players being right handed. As the ball is being thrown in, the guard does not rush to the receiver, that would cause her to pass off immediately. You want her to dribble enabling you to trap. The guard covering the ball should stay even with the ball so the trap cannot be broken. The weakside

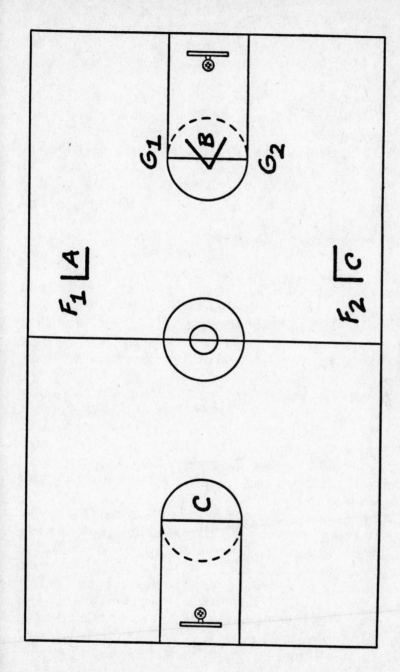

Diagram 7-14

guard patrols through the middle preventing a cross-court pass. The strong side forward stays at midcourt until the ball is two or three steps away and then moves up quickly to set the trap with the guard. The weakside forward falls into the deep middle to prevent a forward pass.

By forcing the ball to the outside, as in man-to-man play, your team has more time to get into position for proper full court coverage. You should never allow an opponent to break a trap with the dribble. They will want to split it. Keep the feet apart with a wide stance and hands high. This cuts down the mobility and view of the ball handler. Traps are used to cause a poor, low percentage pass—usually a lob—that can be intercepted. Any pass intercepted should be advanced immediately to your basket. Don't wait for the rest of the team to come down and set up.

The weakside players should break for the basket and expect a possible pass. Because you have taken the ball from your opponent, they will hesitate to think about the turnover, and you should take advantage of that transition hesitation to score. If you hesitate, you give the opponent an opportunity to play defense. Further if you can convert a few early turnovers, it has a demoralizing effect on your opponent.

In teaching the 2-2-1, begin by having only two people work offensively against it. Require that they dribble into the trap, predominantly using the right side of the floor. Whistle play dead as the trap occurs to check player position on the floor. It should look like Diagram 7-15. It is important to remember that this is a zone, and it is played like a zone, each player having an area of responsibility.

Gradually add a third, fourth and fifth offensive player. Do not give any clues to the offense as to how to advance the ball up the floor. Breaking the press is a separate offensive lesson; you are working on defense.

The point at which the press is broken is on the first *forward* pass or if the ball is dribbled to the half court line. A backward or lateral pass in the back court is not a breaking pass and players should continue to pursue the ball, trying to set traps. When dropping into their zone because the press has

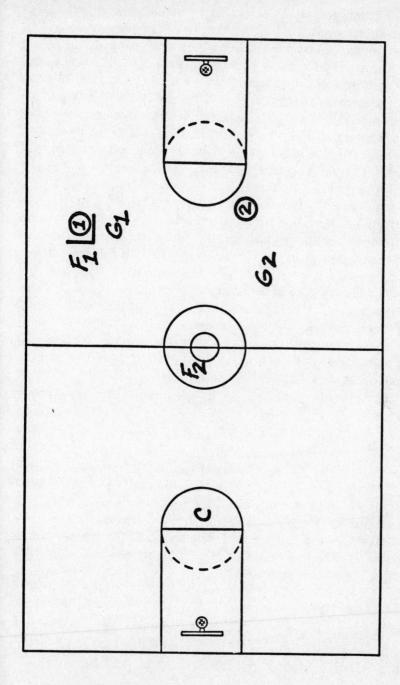

Diagram 7-15

been broken, the players should run backwards, not turn their backs on the ball. All steps taken in floor coverage should be slide steps, not crossovers. Both backward running and slide or shuffle steps can be used in warm-ups. We run many backward and shuffle steps in practice daily. The shuffles are run criss-cross (Diagram 7-16). Players are asked to take a guard stance and keep it throughout the run. More than three times on a full sized floor is inhuman. If you stress conditioning, and want to use this for conditioning and practicing of steps, try it yourself to see how difficult three full trips back and forth up the court are.

The guards, in learning the press, have a tendency to rush the ball handler rather than allowing the trap to occur. They must become actors and appear to be passive while the dribbler gets herself into position so the trap can take place. The forwards have a tendency to come up to the ball too quickly. However, that problem is corrected as you add offensive people. A few passes, especially through the middle, keep the weakside players area-conscious rather than ball-conscious. Keep an eye on the center or the person you chose to place deep. She will get bored waiting for the action to come to her and she may wander toward it. She must stay in her zone.

2-2-1 Zone Press Switch

A variation of the 2-2-1 zone press is the switch (Diagram 7-17). G_2 sets up first and then rushes towards the inbounds passer. G_1 slides to the middle of the lane after G_2 has made her move. Once the pass is made inbounds, the same area coverage applies as in the 2-2-1 zone press. This variation is successful if the 2-2-1 is being broken up the middle. G_1 becomes a prime interceptor, which causes the pass to go to the sidelines thereafter if indeed you do intercept because the steal gives you an instant layup.

3-1-1 Zone Press

A zone press that is ideal for beginning a game because it applies immediate pressure to the ball is the 3-1-1 (Diagram 7-18). Your opponent is not loosened up at the beginning of a

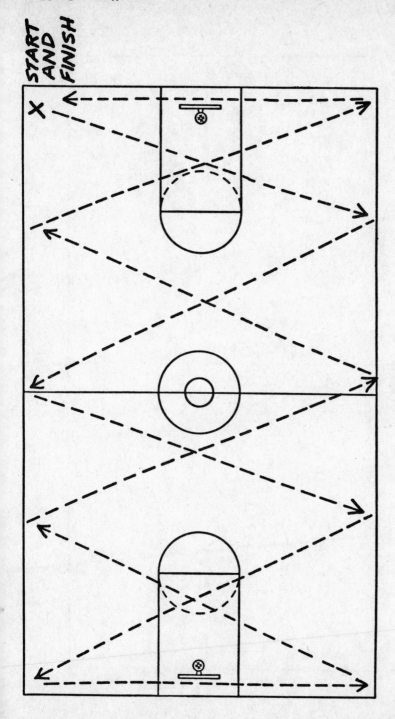

Diagram 7-16

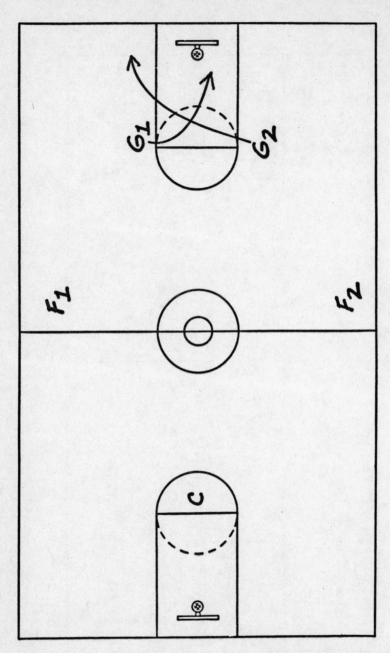

Diagram 7-17

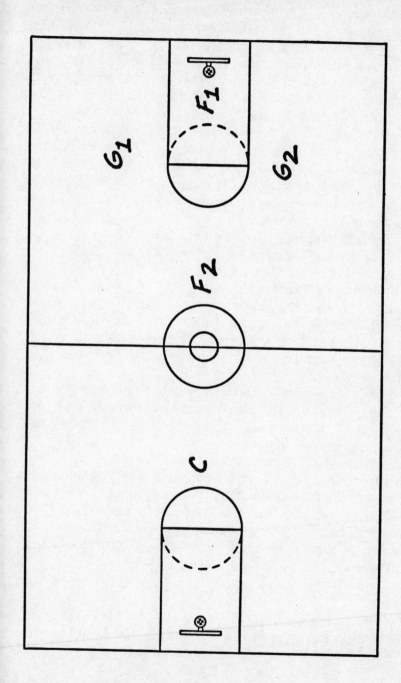

Diagram 7-18

game. It takes a few trips up and down the floor to get into the flow of the game. You can take advantage of the tightness they experience and set a tone of aggressiveness within your team.

The up forward and ball side guard trap the first pass inbounds. The weakside guard drops back to cut off a forward passing lane to the middle. The deep forward anticipates the next move depending on the placement of the opponents. The center swings back and towards the side of the floor the ball is on (Diagram 7-19). The deep forward is responsible for any easy break away basket on the side opposite the center. The working together on defense between F_2 and C can be practiced by three-on-two work, starting just before the mid court line and moving to the basket.

The first trap tries to keep the ball deep in the back court. You are encouraging a pass backward or laterally. The time element becomes the major factor. If you can keep the ball deep in the backcourt through strong harassment on the ball, after five or six seconds your opponent will have a tendency to rush a pass forward to beat the ten-second rule. Your roving weakside guard or the deep forward become prime intercepters. Again turn the play around and run it in for a score.

The 3-1-1 requires your opponent to think forward and sidelines. If they go to neither area immediately they are playing into your hands—often literally. This defense, if used aggressively on the ball as soon as it is passed inbounds, often yields several early errors because the players are cold. Work on layups so you can covert their turnovers. Because you employ it at the start of the game, you can jump out to a quick 8 or 10 point lead and often your opponent hasn't even reached mid court. Expect your opponent to call timeout and be prepared to change to a different press to counteract her adjustments.

1-1-2-1 Zone Press

An excellent press to change to is the 1-1-2-1 (Diagram 7-20). It puts pressure on the ball being thrown inbounds, which the 3-1-1 did not. In the 3-1-1 you allowed the ball to be

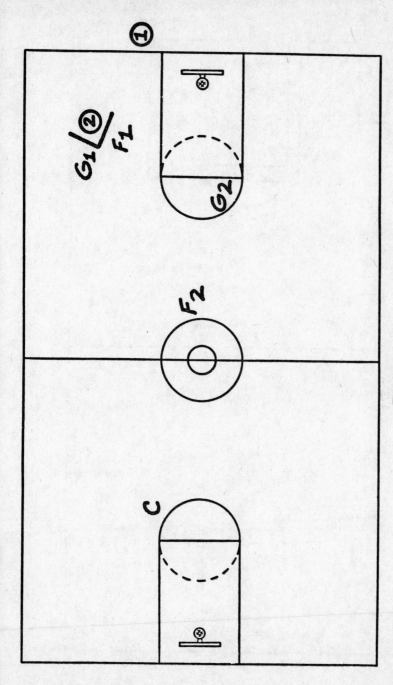

Diagram 7-19

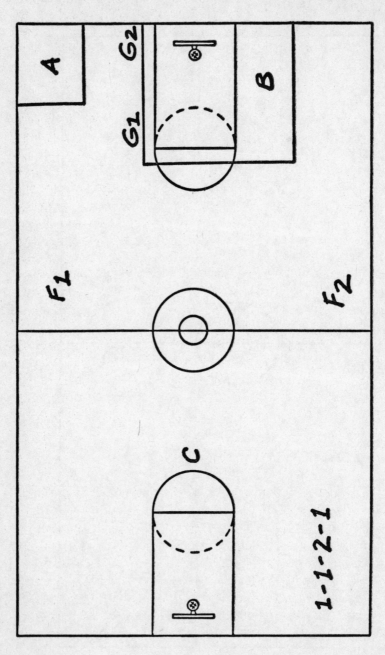

Diagram 7-20

thrown inbounds. With the 1-1-2-1 you add that pressure and cover the areas that were previously open, giving different areas to which your opponent can throw the ball. If their instructions to break the 3-1-1 were followed however, they will be throwing the ball to you. The shaded areas in Diagram 7-21 showing the open areas to pass to against a 3-1-1 are in contrast to those that are shaded in Diagram 7-22, the open areas of the 1-1-2-1. What was open in the 3-1-1 is well covered in the 1-1-2-1, hence you start with the 3-1-1 and switch to the 1-1-2-1.

The defensive coverage in the 1-1-2-1 is similar to the 2-2-1 except for the movement of the guards in the back court. G_2 pressures the ball, leaving areas A and B open. G_1 moves directly to the ball if it is thrown in either of these areas. After the initial thrown-in pass, G_2 moves to the area without the ball. Again the overplay principle is used by the guard on the ball with the objective of moving the ball along the sideline to an eventual trap with the forward. Once the pass is made inbounds and the guards have assumed their areas of responsibility, the 1-1-2-1 is played like the 2-2-1.

To begin your season the 2-2-1 and the 3-1-1 are adequate to give the full court pressure you desire. As the season progresses you can add the variations possible but it is more important that the team know the two defenses well before moving on to others. The use of these presses will give your team the reputation of being aggressive, a psychological advantage if your opponent does not employ them.

TEACHING PRESSES EVEN IF YOU NEVER USE THEM

With the tremendous success of zone presses, as best witnessed in the unmatched record of the UCLA men's team in tournament victories through the John Wooden era, more and more teams are employing them. Therefore, teams must be prepared to break the presses. The best way to teach your team how to break a press is to teach them how to play it. Once the team understands the philosophy of what the press

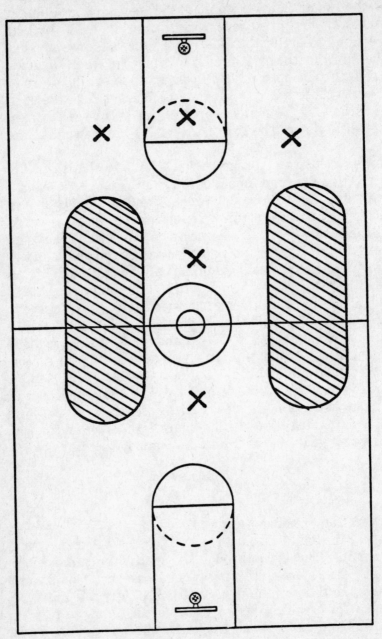

Diagram 7-21

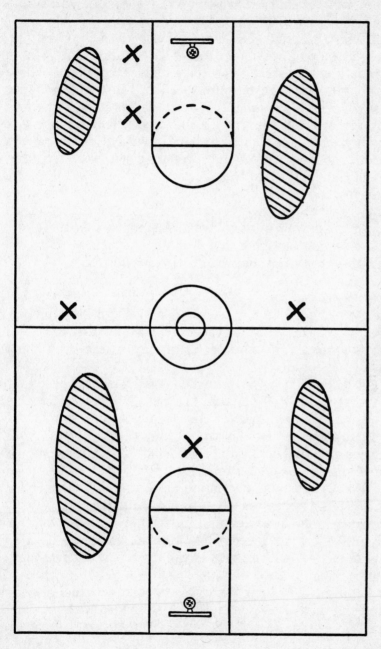

Diagram 7-22

is attempting to do, they can recognize where the vulnerable areas are.

Keeping in mind that every defense gives up something and each has weaknesses, it is necessary to understand where the weaknesses are that you can take advantage of and where the strengths are that you want to avoid. The key to breaking presses is a series of quick, accurate passes to the basically uncovered areas of the floor. A talented dribbler can break them but not consistently or continuously; therefore you should try to apply the team concept of basketball, involving many of your players in the effort.

In looking at the 2-2-1 press, the best place to break it, getting the ball quickly, efficiently up the floor is seen in Diagram 7-23. You want to avoid the trap areas; therefore, you do not want to dribble there. X_1 inbounds to X_2, preferably your center or strong forward. She turns toward the basket and passes to either X_1 or X_3. X_2 then moves down the middle of the floor receiving the pass back. X_2 does not dribble but passes to either X_1 or X_3. After this series of passes the ball should be near midcourt. Because the passes are more lateral than forward, the defense tends to stay in the back court following the ball.

As the ball nears mid court, X_4 and X_5 should break for the basket and look for a pass. You will then have a possible two-on-one situation to go in for a score. After two or three successful baskets against this press, you will force your opponent to fall back, call a timeout for adjustments, or change to a three-quarter or half-court press.

If you can completely eliminate the dribble, you will need no more than four passes to get the ball into scoring position. Remember that a dribble is no more than a pass to oneself. Four passes obviously take less time to complete than 15 passes to oneself and you take advantage of the defense being out of position.

Against a 3-1-1 the open areas are along the sidelines and behind the front three defenders. The shaded areas in Diagram 7-24 show exactly where you want to pass the ball. Again X_2 should be a player with above average height

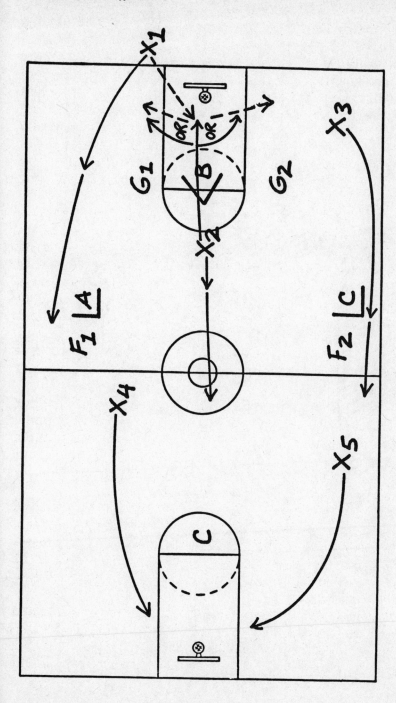

Diagram 7-23

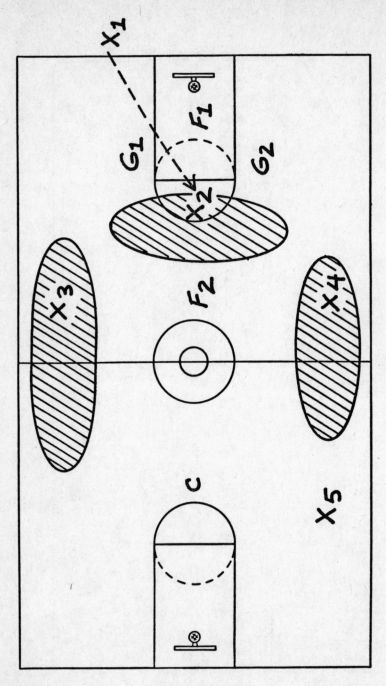

Diagram 7-24

because you must pass over the first line of defense. X_2 can pass to either X_3 or X_4. On defense, the center is suppose to swing to the ball side. If you go to X_3 she can pass directly to X_5 for a back door score. With three passes you have broken this press.

To break the 1-1-2-1, employ the same attack you used against the 2-2-1 except X_3 should set up beyond the free-throw line rather than behind it (Diagram 7-25). X_2 can then pass to X_3 using a good pivot turn. X_3 can pass back to X_2 as in the break against the 2-2-1. This lateral movement of the ball tends to hold the defensive forwards in the back court allowing X_4 and X_5 to again have two-on-one play against the center.

The 2-2-1 switch zone press (Diagram 7-17) is designed to stop this easy break that you can use against the 2-2-1 or 1-1-2-1. It allows the defense to throw a player, G_1, in front of your receiver of the inbounds pass, X_2, and she can intercept. Your counteraction to the switch is for your center to make her move forward as a decoy. The inbounds pass will go to either guard, but the action thereafter should again be down the middle of the floor. The middle is the most direct route, and it will provide for you many opportunities to outnumber your opponent in the front court.

USING THE LONG PASS AS A LAST RESORT

In looking at all of the offensive attacks to break the full court pressure, it is obvious that the long pass to players just beyond the half court line is open. So too are the even longer passes to players in the corners of their front court. To break presses consistently without turnovers you should try to establish your back court break before going to the long ball. If you can work the back court well, the defensive players in the mid court will move up towards the action. Their movement will then give you the two-on-one baskets by utilizing the deeper offensive players with the long pass.

The ability of a team to play the presses is of equal importance to its ability to break them. While talent alone in

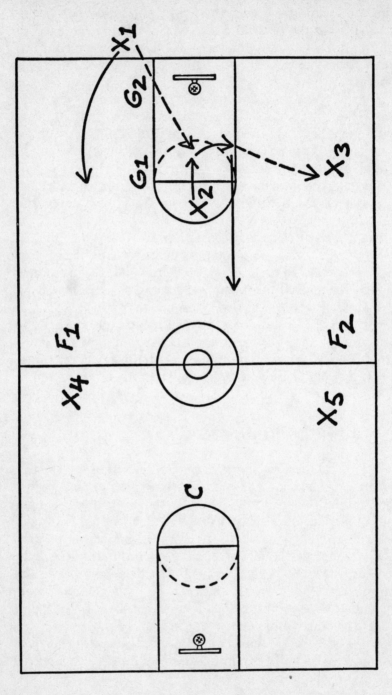

Diagram 7-25

the hands of an adept dribbler can be the answer, team play based on the philosophy of floor coverage and general weaknesses provides a smooth break with a low risk of turnovers. While your team may not be proficient in their press plays, they will better handle them if they know how to play them, because they will understand their purpose and intent. Part of that understanding includes the desire to have the opponent crowd in the back court, allowing your people to be free in your front court. Continued long passes will simply back up the defense, thereby denying your chances for two-on-one play. Hold your long passes as long as possible. If you can hold your long passes until you are near mid court, you can better work the open corners in the front court with your two deep people taking their lone center who is back. This is best accomplished by working your way down court through the middle with lateral passes. That three-player wave coming down the floor attracts the attention of the pressing defense and gives you the opening for the longer passes when you want them, not the desperation kind your opponent hopes to cause.

8

SPECIAL SITUATION PLAYS
MAKE THE DIFFERENCE

The most ignored aspect of women's basketball is the special situation plays, jump balls, and out-of-bounds, yet these very plays are the offensive attacks that can make the difference, make you a winner. You should approach the special situations with simplicity and aggressiveness, especially aggressiveness. In these moments of the game, players relax briefly, hesitate and often become confused, stepping out of their comfortable, well-known roles. Your purpose should be to teach your team the plays from the technical aspect as well as emotional or attitude aspect. In all cases, the plays are specific and direct.

OUT-OF-BOUNDS VS. THE FULL COURT PRESS

Occasionally you will encounter a man-to-man full court press during a game but it is difficult to play for an entire game because it is difficult to play physically for the players and very conducive to fouling. A coach may elect to begin a game with it to try to confuse you early but generally you will see it in the fourth quarter if a team is behind, and they want to cause turnovers, which they hope to convert to baskets.

If you encounter the man-to-man full court press in the beginning of the game, employ all of your players in the backcourt as in Diagram 8-1.

The inbounds pass is to the center; the center fakes to her left and passes to G_2. The center then moves to the center of the jump circle. G_1 after completing the inbounds pass fakes to her right and moves to the center of the floor and receives a pass from G_2. G_1 dribbles, if possible, to the ten-second line or works with G_2 in passing the ball up the floor. Avoid staying in one area and move forward. Staying in the backcourt takes time and the players tend to become too concerned about the ten-second rule and that is where the turnovers occur, in haste.

One aspect to note on any out-of-bounds work from the backcourt is that over three-fourths of the time the ball is thrown in from the right side of the floor, looking at the offensive basket. After an opponent's score, take the ball out from the left side of the floor. Your opponents have fewer experiences working on that side of the floor. You simply work the play in Diagram 8-1 to the reverse. Put G_2 on the other side of the floor. Either way, G_1 will dribble the ball up the middle.

If your opponent's man-to-man is played very tightly, use the play in Diagram 8-2 to loosen them, which will give you the working room you need to run the play in Diagram 8-1.

G_1's purpose is to throw the long ball to either G_2 or F_1, F_1 being your fastest forward. G_1 must be your strongest throwing guard. The center moves to the ball and F_2 moves to the sideline. They are your outlets. Our experience, however, has been that the sprinters are open because the opponents are unready for the long bomb.

OUT-OF-BOUNDS UNDER YOUR BASKET

In keeping with the approach of directness on all special plays, out-of-bounds under your own basket should reveal the epitome of that attitude. There is no reason for you to be satisfied with just passing the ball inbounds almost to midcourt and then proceeding to run a standard play off an

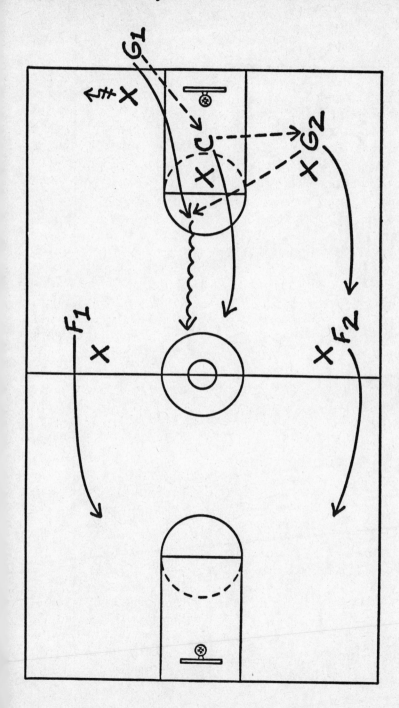

Diagram 8-1

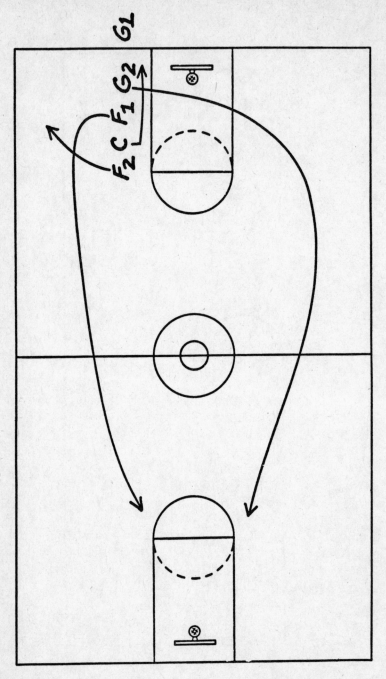

Diagram 8-2

offense. Go immediately to the basket. The fewer people who handle the ball between the inbounds pass and the shot, the better your chances of being successful on the shot. Obviously with fewer ball handling chances, fewer turnovers could occur. Further, you always want to take advantage of that brief defensive lapse that so often occurs in the transition aspect of the game.

In teaching this kind of special play, stress priority of each player capable of receiving the inbounds pass. They rank one through four on each play according to the percentage of the shot they would take. Our most successful play over three seasons has stood without any adjustments even though we played the same opponents in a conference twice a year.

Diagram 8-3 not only shows the players' routes but also numbers them by priority from the point of view of the inbounds passer. F_1 is looked at first; she would have a simple layup. F_2 would also have a layup. C would have a 3-4 foot jump shot. G_2 is always open if the other three are covered, and she is to take an immediate jump shot. We ask G_1 to trail to the outside of the play and stay at the top of the key. You will find that after G_2 has popped a few, the defense comes over to cover, which then opens the other three options.

Another special that the players enjoy capitalizes on three players moving to the basket from the free-throw line with the fourth playing Statue of Liberty at the line. Again priority for the inbounds passer is established.

In Diagram 8-4, F_2 is the prime receiver because she is moving towards a layup. F_1 is clear for a jump shot. G_2 would have a jump shot. C stays on the free-throw line when everyone else breaks for the basket. Opponents tend to concern themselves with the movement, leaving C open. She should try to drive in.

The lineup has been a standard special play but our implementation differs from normal execution (Diagram 8-5). F_2 moves directly to the ball. If she receives it she puts up a short turnaround jump shot. C has a layup. F_1 takes a corner jumper. G_2 is generally left alone, again to penetrate the middle.

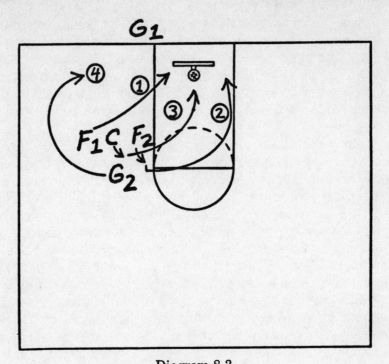

Diagram 8-3

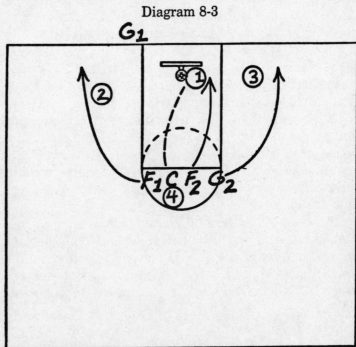

Diagram 8-4

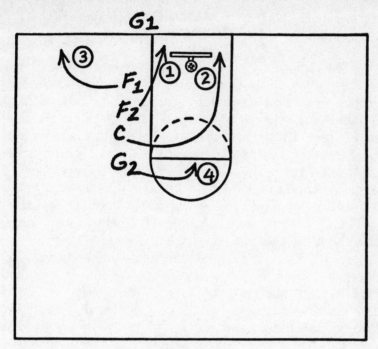

Diagram 8-5

In all of these plays there are a number of points the players should learn along with the movements. The shot should be immediate, or you will have a three-seconds-in-the-lane violation. If your opponent shows you a man-to-man rather than zone as a defense, go inside. In each case you are putting your height inside. It gives you rebounding strength for the second shot, and you are penetrating each time. Aggressiveness is the key.

On all of these plays we do not initiate the movement with a ball slap. It not only signals your team; it also tells the defense that things are going to happen right now. We instruct our G_1 to take her time getting to the inbounds spot while the rest of the team hustles to their places on the floor. G_1 calls the code name of the play she wants as soon as the official indicates the ball is ours. When she takes the ball from the official, the players make their moves. There is no warning to the defense.

OUT-OF-BOUNDS ON SIDELINE
IN YOUR FRONT COURT

The philosophy of special plays stays the same no matter where you are on the floor. Be aggressive. Move to the basket. When you are on the sideline in your front court, don't be satisfied with throwing the ball towards midcourt. It's not easy to score from there. To get to the basket you will probably need three or four people handling the ball. By the time you get to the basket, you have given the defense more than adequate time to set up.

In Diagram 8-6 F_1 comes across the lane, receives the ball and takes a turnaround jump shot. G_2 fakes to the corner and cuts back to the basket receiving a pass over her right shoulder. Don't pass to the inside, left shoulder, because of the interception possibility. G_2 should put the ball on the floor and take a jump shot. F_2 cuts across the lane to rebounding position. C stays home and is the outlet if G_2 and F_1 are covered. One pass, a shot and a high probability of success all

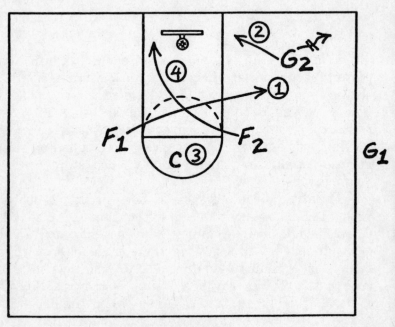

Diagram 8-6

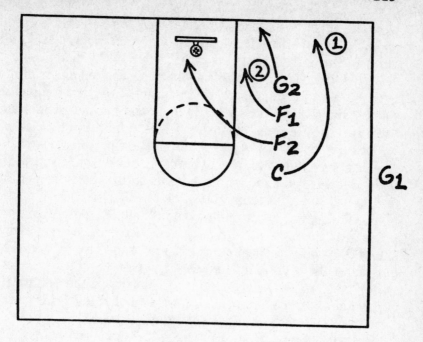

Diagram 8-7

exist because you are attacking. Teams don't expect that immediacy of action thrown at them. They expect a conservative, patient process. The unexpectedness of action often leads to defensive fouls as the players try to react to stop the shot.

In Diagram 8-7, G_2 serves as a screen for C who takes a jump shot. F_1 has a turnaround jumpshot. F_2 moves to a rebounding position. This play, like the others, is simple and quick, and those are the keys to its effectiveness.

SCORING OFF THE JUMP BALL

While jumping ability is stressed in basketball through conditioning, exercises and even specialized equipment, jumping with a purpose is not emphasized. Yet for jumping in any phase of the game to be worthwhile it must have a purpose. Jump ball plays emphasize the point.

The effort to get the possession on jump ball plays seems to be helter-skelter. In jump after jump players are seen tapping the ball around purposelessly. With specific plays designed to move directly to a shot as opposed to being content with merely gaining control of the ball, the players jump with greater purpose. With specific plays, the jumper knows she has a specific direction toward which she should work. Each of her teammates knows she too has a specific route to work.

Diagram 8-8 shows the play we have used repeatedly both to open quarters and after tie balls. For the opening jump, X_1 is our center. Thereafter on the tie balls, X_1 takes the place of whoever is jumping except X_3. If X_3 is jumping, X_5 takes her place on the circle and X_1 becomes the defensive safety. X_3 is our quickest guard; X_5 our other guard; X_2 and X_4 our forwards. If X_2 is left-handed, the play can hardly miss.

X_1 taps to X_2. X_3 breaks for the basket on the toss of the ball for the jump as allowed in high school rules. She doesn't have to wait for the tap as in college. X_2 passes to X_3 who goes in for the layup. This play is successful even when the opponents put a defender back in their own free-throw circle.

X_2 breaks for the basket after the pass, often creating two-on-one situations. If X_2 is left-handed, you gain the advantage of having the pass off to the side of the opponents around the circle in that area as opposed to over them. The chances for an interception are decreased.

Diagram 8-9 is the overload jump ball scoring play. Again you are attempting a quick, aggressive play with an immediate shot with minimal ball handling.

If we have a height advantage with the jumpers (jumping height—not necessarily physical height), we send X_2 and X_3 down on the toss and tap to X_5. X_2 and X_3 work to the left side of the floor. X_5, who gets the tapped ball, dribbles quickly to that area where the defender on the baseline would be in a 2-1-2, 1-2-2 or 3-2 zone.

X_5 can shoot off a screen set by X_3 on the defender, with X_5 making her move to the midway point of the free-throw lane. X_5 can also pass to X_2 who makes her move along the baseline working off a screen set by X_3. X_1 is the rebounder on the weakside of the floor. X_4 is the defensive safety. To be success-

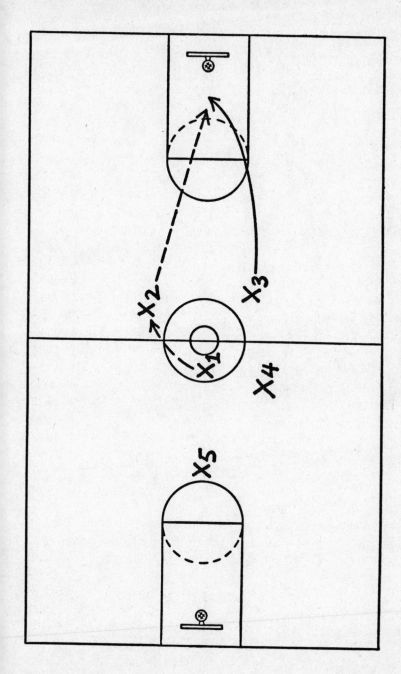

Diagram 8-8

Diagram 8-9

ful the play must be executed immediately. Don't give the defense time to set.

Girls' basketball has a significant number of jump balls in each game. Having specific plays that emphasize direct routes to the basket with quick shots, you can gain a scoring advantage. These easy shots are not easily matched by an opponent who is only satisfied with gaining possession from the jump. (This jump ball information is taken from "Scoring Off the Jump Ball," by Dorothy A. Guiliani, *Women's Coaching Clinic,* October, 1977 pp.25-27.)

Regardless of how well you practice your jump ball plays, the possibility always exists that you won't win the jump. Because you are concentrating on the jump ball play, you don't want to emphasize the negative defensive recovery aspects should you fail to get the ball. However the team should always be prepared for that possibility.

If you lose the jump ball effort, instruct your team to fall back into a nice, safe zone, preferably the 2-1-2 or 2-3. It will close the lane to any easy breakaway basket. The activity following a jump ball is transition basketball, a changing from offense to defense or vice versa. If your transition to defense is slow because your team is trying to pick up their player responsibilities from man-to-man, one offensive player can be left open for the brief time it takes to get her the ball, and she can score. It is important to have the access lanes to the basket covered, and a zone will do that for you.

DEFENDING THE OUT-OF-BOUNDS PLAY

Never, never, never use a player-to-player defense against an out-of-bounds play on the front court of your opponent or under their basket. You are practically giving away two points. The chances of covering the land and key areas are almost impossible. Use a zone that has a broader baseline coverage. For example, the 1-3-1 still gives away too much of the baseline. The 2-1-2 usually gives you the security you need; a 2-3 also gets the job done.

Having used a few trick plays and also having seen a few, I've learned to tell the players to take their originally designed places and not to move until the ball is in the air entering the inbounds area. Trick delays or crossing patterns should be ignored until the ball is in the air. Know where the ball is when you are defensing an out-of-bounds under their basket. With zone play you will have the plays in the highest shooting percentage areas covered.

THE STALL AND FREEZE ARE DEFENSES

The stall and freeze are invaluable tools to have in your repertoire of options to use during a game. While generally considered part of the offensive arsenal, they can be viewed as defenses because their purpose is to prevent your opponent from scoring. As long as you have the ball, your opponent can't score. They do not have to be saved for the end of the game. There are times during a game when you will want to employ them. If your opponent makes several successive scores that you haven't answered, a slow down can take their momentum from them without using a timeout. If you have to use a timeout every time you want to make a change, you are wasting them. Get some coding keys for your stalls and communicate them to your captain.

Another time you may want to use a stall is at the beginning of the second half. Your opposing mentor has just spent five minutes telling her team what changes are needed. By using a stall, you completely change the thinking and plans of your opponent. Further, if they have no success disrupting your stall, you will force her to call a timeout to make the needed adjustments. In a close game, forcing your opponent to use timesout is as valuable as scoring. At the end of the game with a minute left she would prefer to have as many as possible, but you force her to use them when she would rather not.

One of the keys to success in bench coaching is to save your timeouts, but force your opponent to use hers. In a tight game you will have the latitude in the closing minutes to make adjustments through the use of a timeout while your opponent can only communicate to her team by yelling out orders from the bench. The use of these special situations such as a stall to start a half may cause your opponent to call a timeout when she really doesn't want to. This kind of strategy pays off in the long run.

9

POLISHING YOUR OFFENSES
AND
DEFENSES IN MID-SEASON

By mid-season your basic offenses and defenses should be established. Nothing fancy or clever has to be accomplished and preferably they should not be fancy. It is more to your advantage to concentrate on fundamentals in the first half of the season. Passing, dribbling, and rebounding should be stressed to the point where they are as close to being instinctive as is humanly possible. While you employ a multiplicity of drills, these basic fundamentals must be stressed. To continuously give away the ball without any real effort or cause by the opponent results in losses. While the continuation of fundamentals work is a must throughout the season, by midseason the emphasis of work being done should shift to polish and the sophistication of offenses and defenses.

DEVELOPING SOPHISTICATION

As stated in Chapter Four, simplicity in developing an offense while you stress defense and fundamentals will keep you in a competitive position at the beginning of the season.

However, if you are a member of a league or conference, you will most often have to play the members twice. Staying with the same simple plays will take away your ability to challenge the opponents. You become too predictable. You cannot allow a team to be completely prepared for you because of one meeting. For that second meeting in the season, you should be able to show some new wrinkles for which the opponents are not prepared. Further, if you want to grow as a team, you cannot rest on past accomplishments, regardless of how successful you may have been.

In Chapter Four, the mobile midpost was introduced. The options discussed show a simple, yet penetrating offense. However, it will not carry you through an entire season. It can remain your staple but add a secondary offense. An overload or an odd front may be your choice. This kind of offense should have fewer options but should include more movement of the players without the ball.

An overload can be chosen if your opponents are traditionally known for zone defenses. You want to use an offense that concentrates effort on specific zones in the defense. If an opponent uses zones predominantly it is either because the players are weak in individual defensive skills or they lack the speed and mobility to go one-on-one with you. If you can bother them enough with an overload, you can either force them to go to a player-to-player defense or be secure in knowing that you will win because they choose to stay with a zone that can't stop you.

AN OVERLOAD OFFENSE

An example of an overload you can use is in Diagram 9-1. X_1 passes to X_2 and cuts through the lane. X_2 immediately passes to X_3. X_3 can pass to X_1 who is cutting through the lane and who would take a jump shot from 6 to 8 feet, or a layup if X_4 can draw the defender she has in her area away from the basket. X_3 can hold the ball and pass to X_2 who is the next cutter and would have the same shot options as X_1. X_3 can also shoot from the corner. If X_3 is consistently successful from the

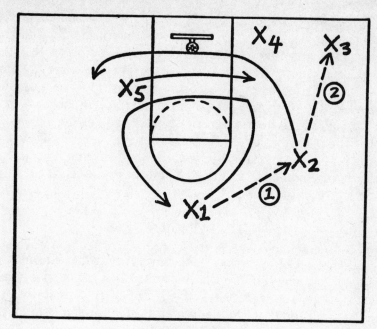

Diagram 9-1

corner, she is sure to draw a defender out, causing X_4 to be open. If X_2 does not receive the pass, X_5 cuts across the lane from the weakside towards X_3. X_5 can receive the pass and take a turnaround jumper. Once the defense starts creeping to the strong side of the floor to cover the majority of shot options, X_5 will be open as the offense goes to work and the initial pass from X_1 can go directly to X_5 in her original position. X_5 would try to drive in for a layup as a back door play. There is a high probability of drawing a foul here because the defense is reacting, not acting. The baseline defender has to make a choice as to whom she is going to cover, and she can't cover everyone in her area.

AN ODD FRONT OFFENSE: THE 1-3-1

A good example of an odd front offense that can be used as a second offense against both zones and player-to-player is the 1-3-1.

X_1 can throw to any of the three in the second line of the offense. If X_3 receives the pass, she can pass to X_5 who has a shot with any fake employed. X_3 can also pass to X_4 who is cutting to the basket. If X_3 or X_4 receive the pass, X_1 cuts to the side of the floor she passes to, as close to X_3 as possible to lose her defender, and goes in for a layup. X_5 must move to the weakside of the floor when the pass goes to either wing. That is, if the pass goes to X_2, X_5 moves across the lane clearing the area for X_1 to come through with the ball. X_2 and X_3 join X_5 for the triangle rebound position. X_4 moves to the top of the key as a safety (Diagram 9-2).

THE SWING OFFENSE

Another offense that has success against both zones and player-to-player defenses is the swing. While it probably has a well-known name in basketball circles (not that I've ever learned it even though I've seen it used by several teams), give

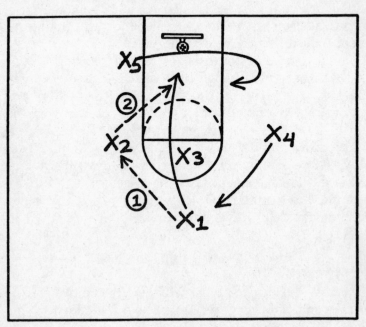

Diagram 9-2

it your own name. Players enjoy naming their own plays; the personalizing creates a motivational force in that they take great pride in doing well in what is exclusively theirs. We had a difficult inbounds play that the team preferred to use and work on because they had affectionately called it "Gobble." Any other name or coded key would have made it an ordinary play, but they identified with it because of their name which had a special meaning to them. A school activity at Thanksgiving, namely a "gobbling" contest, generated the name. For example, if you are the Spartans, this can be the "Spartan Swing" (Diagram 9-3).

X_1 passes to X_3; X_3 passes to X_2 who has cut across the lane (swings across). X_2 can: take a turnaround jump shot, pass to X_3 on a give-and-go, pass to X_5 who moves up along the side of the lane, or pass to X_1 for a back door play. The keys to success are that the wings must start wide, causing the defense to spread, and the choices by X_2 must be made predominantly to her side of the floor before X_1 can be a

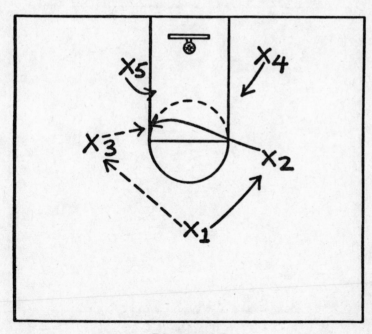

Diagram 9-3

successful back door. She wants to draw the defense around her so a few successful jump shots and give-and-gos must be made early in the attack (Diagram 9-4).

X_1 fakes a pass to X_3, causing X_2 to swing left. X_1 then dribbles wide to wing area just vacated by X_2. X_4 fakes outside and moves outside and moves up to a midpost area on the lane and receives the pass from X_1. X_4 can: take a turnaround jump shot, pass to X_2 on an outside give-and-go, or pass to X_3 at the free-throw line.

In both of these efforts, the plays can be reversed to the opposite side of the floor and in both you have good rebounding position. If the defense starts anticipating the passes to the wings, keep them honest by having X_1 drive the lane or run a give-and-go with the wings and point guard working together if the defense bottles up the area by sagging to the ball when your swing wing gets the ball.

Any of these offenses can be added at midseason because they are not so difficult that they need weeks of work, and yet

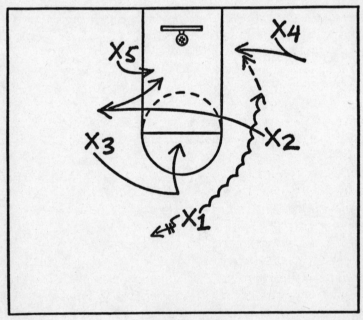

Diagram 9-4

they are quite different from the mobile midpost. These offenses are not drastic changes in that they maintain the attacking, aggressive approach to offense. Their intent is to send the ball to the basket with minimal ball handling and limited movement yet they look different. Hence, they cause your opponent to give some new thinking about how your team will be stopped. Without a great deal of effort, you can present a versatile offensive punch. It gives you the option of an offensive attack if your opponent changes defenses. You will have a choice of offenses to change game pace, which we will discuss later.

STRESSING REBOUNDS WITH STATS

One of the areas of the game too often taken for granted is the rebound. An old adage of "control the backboard, control the scoreboard," is a good lesson to inculcate in your players. While you may take time in practice to work on rebounding with the triangle rebounding drill, tipping drills and the use of rebound equipment, nothing drives the point home like a thorough examination of game stats. The variety of combinations of stats from all of the games in the first half of the season should be examined closely by the entire team. Keeping the stats a deep, dark secret, well hidden in Athletic Department files accomplishes nothing. One of the points you must remember throughout a season is that not only do you want a physically functioning team, but you also want a mentally functioning team. Winning teams are made up of intelligent, thinking players, not robots that can be turned on and off at will. Intelligence in basketball doesn't relate to IQ scores but to the players' ability to analyze the game. Use some of your practice time for teaching the game, not just for coaching. Analyzing stats is part of that teaching.

By using the stats sheets in Chapter Two, you can show the players the relationship between rebounds, shots taken, and shooting percentages. There will be some obvious examples where either you or your opponent has been blown out of a game. Rebounds are 80 to 40, shots are predominantly inside or outside and shooting percentages range from 8% to 68%. My team has had these kinds of examples. If you have twice the rebounds that your opponents have, you force them to shoot a phenomenally high percentage to win. To attain that high percentage, they need a can't-miss-kid from 20 feet or they must be penetrating, getting the easy, short inside shot. If they are hitting consistently, but you control your offensive boards, getting two and three shots each time down the floor, you don't have to match that high shooting percentage to stay in the game. In my years of coaching, in only one game did we control the boards and lose the game. We shot 8%!.

In close games you can show the players the quarters in which they controlled the boards and the relationship to the scoring. How many shots did the opponent get each time down the floor? If you can hold your opponent to one, you give yourself far more latitude in terms of the overall game. Rebounding is team effort, more easily taught and learned than shooting and all players can contribute. When a guard takes eight boards in a game, it isn't necessarily true that she got all long outside caroms. She, in some instances, was a cutter inside who did a good job blocking out and did some jumping, not just reaching. A 5′4″ guard who develops jumping ability and blocking out ability can be just as effective as a 5′7″ or 5′8″ forward who reaches.

When you stress rebounds, those abilities become goals that all the players hope to achieve. In the first practice after a game, begin your session with a review of the game stats. Praise the top three or four rebounders for their efforts. Avoid talking only about scorers. If you want team players, stress the team stats such as rebounds, steals and assists. The newspapers generally take care of the scoring praise for you. Don't completely avoid the scorers because they are obviously a part of the game, but they don't win the game. It is the total effort that shows up in the final stats that wins the game.

GETTING PICKY ON DEFENSE

When you begin the season you stress fundamentals. Strong fundamentals win games throughout the entire season. They can never be practiced too much, yet to continuously work on them creates boring practices. Further, the players want more than the basics. They enjoy the challenge of new and difficult facets of the game. Midseason is a good time to begin teaching intricate defensive play.

One area to improve is the zone press. If you have taught the 3-1-1, 2-2-1, and 2-2-1 flex, a more difficult press is the 1-2-2. In Diagram 9-5 the defense is set in its assigned areas, with the offense in hypothetical positions for the sake of explanation. Note that X_2 and X_3 have arrows pointing away from the ball. The players play with their backs to the ball. You have placed X_1, a center or tall forward, in front of the inbounds passer. She should be playing with hands high, forcing a high pass inbounds. X_2 and X_3 are playing almost man-to-man against the two possible receivers. Eyes, arms, hands, and feet can be used in a fake but the waist can't. X_2 and X_3 move with the receivers in the backcourt, watching their waists.

If O_1 throws long, it must be a high pass to get over X_1's arms. This lob can be intercepted by X_4 or X_5. To break this press, you force the opponent to bring everyone to the backcourt to outnumber your defenders. That keeps the ball in the backcourt where you can use traps to force other lob passes or held balls. You have an opportunity for possession in either situation.

Another aspect of defense that can be improved upon in midseason is the controlling of an individual opponent's floor position. In the area around the top of the circle your defenders should work on overplaying the offense to the degree that the offense is forced where you want them to be. Stress that the overplay is done with the feet, not arms. In practice have the ball handler dribble strong towards one side of the floor. It is the defender's job to force her to the other side of the floor. You may want to protect a player in foul trouble during a game, and this defensive maneuver will allow you to do so.

While your players have been taught to deny passes by midseason they should be fairly proficient at it. Now is the time to start timing them. Can all four off the ball stay with their players thirty seconds? The extended period of denial

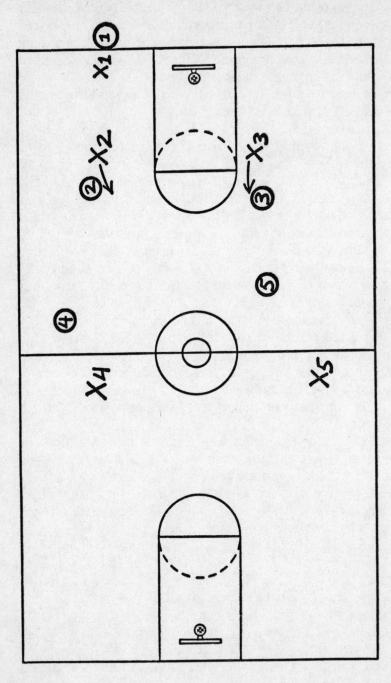

Diagram 9-5

should be employed as often as possible but particularly at the end of quarters and the end of a game.

PREPARING FOR THE SECOND HALF
OF THE SEASON

You have added another offense and stressed more specific work on defense, but you aren't ready for the second half of the season until you have dealt with the mental, emotional and psychological parts of the game. Not only must you deal with those areas in the players but also with yourself.

Seasons can be very long. The day-after-day practices drain you emotionally. If you try to be too methodical in your practices, motivation of players declines. On the other hand, if much cheering occurs in the beginning of the season, it is difficult to maintain a high level of that emotion over a season. Your job is to try to find a balance that is comfortable for you and the players that rests between these two extreme practice environments.

Analyze your own position. Are you getting a little tired of daily practices? Is getting high for a game becoming more difficult? How is the season going? If you have having great success, is your team getting overconfident about playing all those same conference foes a second time? If you have been losing consistently, are the players assuming a losing attitude?

Look realistically at what you have exactly. How do you answer the above questions? Often a coach assesses her team's position; rarely does she ask the team. However, it is a good experience for the players to make their own appraisal of the team. If I have a talkative group, we have a rap session in practice when everyone's view is welcome. With a quiet team, I have asked the players to write what they think are the strengths and weaknesses of the team and what they think we could do to improve. Expect the Hawthorne effect to be present to some degree. Look beyond that to the criticism that has been stated. In subsequent practices explain that the reason you are doing something is because some of the players indicated a need for it and that you have agreed with their appraisal.

This head-on look at the team by you and the players may bring to light problems that you may not know of. The players, for example, might think you are giving special treatment to one or two (the old favoritism problem) which may be real or imagined, and you will find out in the exchange of ideas. Any problems that are nonskill oriented should be eliminated as soon as possible. This midseason meeting of the minds is a great opportunity to let them all surface and be dealt with. Be realistic though; not all problems will be solved. You can have players who are pessimists or negative thinkers. If they've been like that for sixteen years, the probability of you changing them during a basketball season is very small. The best you can hope for is that their attitude doesn't become prevalent within the team.

Finally, discuss your preseason goals. If they now seem unrealistic, be honest enough to say so and set some that are attainable. If you can obviously attain those you set, talk about the importance of working for them and not assuming they will be reached. A good shot of vigor should be instilled in the players. Regardless of what has occurred thus far in the season, give a good positive message of bright, sunny days ahead that can be achieved with everyone's effort and contributions.

10

EMPLOYING STRATEGY
TO SET THE GAME PACE

The most difficult facet of the game for coaches to learn is the strategy, the actual bench coaching. The technical learning can be self-taught with books or by attending clinics. It is much like a foreign language. You can learn the vocabulary, the conjugation of verbs, the agreement of adjectives and nouns with their various endings, and with some practice, you can read the prose under study. The strategy, however, is more like speaking the new tongue. It takes practice and use to master it. Too often coaches wait until actual game conditions to try to learn strategy, which is really the hard way. Strategy in basketball can be practiced and studied as you would study moves for a chess game or bidding in bridge. While every basketball game is different, there are definite patterns. Knowing the patterns allows you to make adjustments in your team's approach that will allow you to set the pace of the game; i.e., play the game the way you decide, not the way your opponent decides.

RECOGNIZING NEEDS FOR DEFENSIVE CHANGES

At the beginning of a game, you have a defense and an offense that you are comfortable with. You've practiced them, the players know them and you feel secure with their execution. In the first quarter, those first few minutes, you should watch your opponent. It is important to recognize as quickly as possible just what your opponent is trying to do offensively. If it appears to be shooting from the outside you may want to change from a zone to man-to-man or to a zone that calls for more aggressiveness from the outside guards such as a triangle-two. If you started with a man-to-man and the opponent has found your weakest defender and is easily driving to the basket, you want to switch to a zone to stop the easy drive in. If your 1-2-2 zone is being picked apart in the middle with a cutter who receives the ball and takes a quick turnaround jump shot, change to a 2-1-2 zone, giving you a defender in the middle of the lane.

Your job in the first quarter is to determine the opponent's main area of attack. Offenses begin a game with plays that have been successful for them. You can make a defensive adjustment early in the game that will reduce their effectiveness. You force them to go to a second choice offensively. They have less confidence, so you are affecting them not only in terms of strategy but also psychologically because they aren't doing what they chose to do.

Try to avoid drastic changes in your defense. Remember the defense you began with was one you felt confident with, so try to keep it but still make the necessary adjustments. If you have opened the game with a 2-1-2 zone and your opponent hits consistently from the shooting area alongside the lane, have one of your guards shift deeper toward the baseline with the weakside guard moving a step past the middle of the lane. The guards should almost be playing man-to-man and trying to deny a pass into the area. Even if a pass is thrown into this area, the denial will force it further outside from the desired shooting spot. This adjustment from the standard zone will give up some shots from the top of the key or from the weakside just to the side of the key but you have taken away one of the opponent's key weapons without entirely scrapping the zone you started with. The psychological effect you have on your opponent by forcing her to make a big change can also cause a negative or defeatist attitude on your team if it is forced to make a big defensive change to try to avoid it. The big defensive move as an element of surprise is good for your team's attitude only if you are winning when it is made or if it has been successful when used in the past in a game that you won. If you are losing, your players may think they are in trouble, so stay with small adjustments as long as possible.

TAKING WHAT THEY GIVE YOU ON OFFENSE

The advantage to having an offensive set such as the previously described mid-post is that it gives you shot options from many places on the floor. When you begin a game you should instruct the team to try several of these options if the opponent is playing zone. By testing several areas of the floor, you can learn a number of things about your opponents quickly. On the first attempted shot from outside, don't watch the shot; watch the rebounding position of your opponents. If you find you can get good offensive rebounding position, you can control your own boards. You can then control the game because you'll get two or three chances to score most times down the floor. It won't hurt to use outside shots with good offensive board follow-up for the second attempt by one of your bigger players inside.

In your early shot attempts watch the defender nearest the ball. Is she flying at the ball when it comes in her area? With the use of fakes you can get her in foul trouble. Watch the defender farthest from the ball. Is she moving from her area of responsibility towards the ball into other defenders' areas? If you see this overplay, leaving part of the area open, call out your code for the weakside play. Fake a pass to the strong side and send a quick pass to the weakside, who can shoot or drive and shoot. The drive and shoot is particularly effective because you can draw a foul from the defender who is out of position and overreacts to get back to her area.

Another common error in playing zone that you should look for is what I call playing "high." The two baseline players in a 2-1-2 zone play towards the key, away from the baseline. Their incorrect position makes the defense appear to be a 2-3 zone. These two should be playing lower to cover the baseline, hence, the word "high." If your opponent is playing high and not covering the baseline, either drive the baseline (again you'll probably draw the foul from the reacting defender) or slide your weakside forward across the baseline underneath the defender and pass in to her. This penetration pass must be quick and accurate. The forward can use the big slide step in for a lay-in.

If your opponent is using a man-to-man defense, your key is movement and penetration. The more movement you can create on offense, the more movement you cause on defense and that will bring you fouls and get you in the bonus early in the game. Against a man-to-man defense you want to clear areas, set picks and drive to the basket. Remember that the closer you get to the basket the higher the percentage of the shot you take. You don't want to make the defender's job easy by shooting from twenty-five feet. Work the ball to get it in around the lane area. It is especially important to have a guard drive in after the big players have cleared the area. You achieve two goals. First you can draw fouls for three point plays and second, you can get relatively easy-looking baskets, which is demoralizing for the opponent.

In looking back through this section, you'll see that fouls have been mentioned several times. You ought not spend all of your effort trying to draw fouls because it works against you. You will either get unwanted offensive charges or even worse the flow of the game is lost with too much individual rather than team play. However, if you look for the defensive errors, you can work in foul conducive areas wherein you can take advantage of the bonus rule. If you can get your opponent in foul trouble early in the game, the game becomes that much easier for you, especially in the final quarter when key players may foul out, tipping the scales of victory your way.

COMING FROM BEHIND

If you are losing by ten or more points every coach will tell you not to try to get it back all at one time. You can only score two points at a time with each offensive attempt down court. But the most neglected factor in coming from behind in a game is defense. Scoring on three or four consecutive trips down court means nothing if you are simply matching baskets with your opponent. You aren't gaining any ground. What is vital is to score, stop your opponent and score again. It sounds easy but how do you achieve it?

Here is a situation where your quarterly shot charts can aid you. Look at the most recent quarter to see where the majority of your opponent's successful shots are made. You seldom find that you are beaten in several areas. Substitute your best defender into the game even if she has little offensive threat. The four other players can do your scoring, but it is crucial to plug the open area that exists for your opponent. If a "star" is beating you, double-team her if necessary. Stop her. You cannot trade baskets and win, so your first job is defense.

If the game is being played at a deliberate pace and is low scoring, change the pace of the game. Your opponent may only be comfortable in a set offense. Pick up the tempo of your offense, even it simply means getting the ball up court faster to get to your own set offense if you don't have fast-break capability. Put pressure on your opponent even it's only a guard-on-guard press to take your opponent out of the comfort of simply dribbling the ball up the floor uncontested.

Another overlooked method of getting back in the game is to go to your bench. You may have predominant height on the floor because you want to control rebounds, but if your opponent is putting on a shooting clinic, there are no rebounds to be had. Get some quickness on the floor to get a hand in the face of the shooters. If you've taught rebounding position to all of your players—and you should, even the tiniest guard—you'll still get your share of the boards.

Contrary to what this section said to begin with, I still find games where it appears we are out of it and we go to the run-and-gun game. It's a desperate move that appears as if you are trying to get it all back at once. However, you'll find there are desperate situations sometimes. In one game we were down by twenty at half time; none of our offenses were working. In the locker room the team was told to scrap all plays and just run and shoot. What resulted was turnovers, fouls, confusion and our getting within two points when time ran out. It's been said a thousand times before, but with one more minute of playing time we would have pulled it out. Our helter-skelter play didn't confuse us but it did cause chaos with the opponents. Their defense fell apart and the timing in their own offense went awry because of the drastically different game being played in the second half.

Coming from behind calls for flexibility on your part. Try to change the game pace, try different players, stress defense and above all remain confident. Show your players with your attitude that it's not ended. If you believe it can be done, they will believe it. If you have to make a drastic change, let it be known that it is to throw the other team into confusion. Don't allow your players to think you are desperate. Desperation is next to giving up. If the desperate move fails, they'll think it's all over but the shouting. Make all the completely different moves necessary throughout the fourth quarter, but always explain them as a means to keep the opponent guessing. Even if you lose, you won't be quitting.

WINNING IN THE FINAL TWO MINUTES

Close games are won in the final two minutes because of coaching decisions. Yes, the players must execute but your decisions are crucial. One of the most important decisions you must make comes early in the game. If the two competing teams appear to be evenly matched, you must decide to save at least two timeouts for the final quarter. It is imperative that you have one timeout for the last minute. Many a game has been lost because in the final minute, with the score tied or a team down by two points, there was no timeout to set the needed strategy to win.

There are obviously many situations in various games that dictate what you do in the final two minutes, but there are some patterns that exist here, too. If you are steadily coming from behind, you can afford to be aggressive because momentum is on your side. If your opponent has no timeouts remaining, go to the hot hand that's been scoring for you and make the play with determination. Don't waste time trying to run down the clock. Your opponent's state of mind is confusion and hope. Confusion about what they should do next and hope that your attempt will fail because they are just trying to hold on to victory while time expires. Your aggressiveness also has a probability of drawing a foul. Unless every player on the floor for the opponent is poised, someone is going to make an error in attempting to hold on to the lead.

PROTECTING THE PLAYER IN FOUL TROUBLE

Besides needing timeouts for the final part of the game, you need your key players. Don't let them foul out in the beginning of the fourth quarter unless you have an equal substitute, which is rare. Knowing when to save players in foul trouble can make the difference going down the home stretch. If a player picks up two fouls in the first quarter, substitute for her. With two she becomes foul-conscious and the third one comes too easily. With three fouls she's in big trouble. By taking her out of the game in the first quarter, you know she can play in the second. If you wait till she picks up the third foul, you are taking a big chance of losing her services to the team for almost an entire quarter.

If a player gets a third foul in the third quarter, substitute. You don't want to risk a fourth that will limit her contributions in the final period. If she must play with four fouls in the early part of the final period, the opponent will very likely attack her area. If she wants to stay in the game, she will not be able to give 100% on defense; she will have to pull back from the offensive threat. Also, she will be less apt to go after a lost ball or rebound wholeheartedly in fear of risking that final foul. If she is the kind of player who doesn't know how to pull back (it's never entered her mind to play anything less than 100%), she will foul out. The rule to remember on fouls then is: SAVE AFTER THREE, NOT FOUR.

If you think that you can't get along without a key player; that is, she is your best shooter, floor leader or only height for the boards, you can protect her in a zone. If you have been playing man-to-man, switch to a zone. Zones are less foul conducive. If you have been playing zone and she is on the outside, move her to the inside of the zone. If she is playing the inside and you believe it is crucial to keep her in the game, then you simply must risk her getting the final fouls. Sometimes you just can't avoid it, but try by all means. You'll need her at the end.

TRADING BASKETS: THE FINAL TRADE

In close games, the fourth quarter often seems to be a case of trading baskets. By that point in the game, you know who your best shooters are that night and you know where the opponent's weaknesses are. What is interesting about basketball is that just as often as you trade baskets, you trade misses. You miss on your offensive attempt and somehow your defense digs in and comes up with the big play denying your opponent on the other end of the floor. You know you are in store for a barn-burner. Regardless of what you try, you can't get that little spurt that gives the moment of comfort. Dig in; it's going down to the final possession.

If you have a two point lead, with thirty seconds left, freeze the ball and run out the clock. If your opponent has the two point lead with thirty seconds remaining, foul and foul fast. Don't wait till there are ten or fewer seconds left on the clock. When you foul, go for the ball, not the body. The free throws will be the one and one bonus instead of two for the intentional foul. (Don't be afraid to plead that case with the officials if the situation is reversed. They won't give it to you on that call, but they very likely will on the next call.) You must foul early, enabling you to have enough time to run the play you want when you get possession. The player to take the shot must be your hot hand that night, not one by reputation, although it may be the same person. Make sure the play you select has good rebounding strength on the weakside of the basket.

If your opponent made her two free throws, call a timeout (if you have one). Call it immediately as the ball goes through the basket. Have a designated player who will run right at the official out-of-bounds. On the throw-in, know specifically who your first and second options are to receive the pass and go right to the hoop. After making the shot, again foul the opponent immediately. At this point you must hope that she misses her free throw. If you get the rebound, pass long to a player on the side of the floor, who in turn passes to a player going to the basket. Make the basket and tie the game. We'll get to overtimes shortly.

If the score is tied in the final minute and you have possession, you want to play for one shot. Unless your team is adept at running the four corner offense, don't go to the spread. Instead pass around the perimeter; that is, set up a little wider than usual or have your point guard and wing work the ball, giving the others time to get to their desired locations to run the play.

Start running the play with about fifteen seconds remaining. The shot should come with six or seven seconds left on the clock. Be sure the play you have chosen has strong rebounding on the weakside. The majority of games won in this tied situation are the result of an offensive rebound being put right back up for the final two points. That is why you take the shot at six seconds; it gives you time for the second try.

PLAYING IN OVERTIME

Nothing turns hair gray faster than an overtime game. The pent-up emotions of an entire game that could have been won several times but wasn't now have to wait for three more minutes to be released. Not only do they wait, but they increase. Overtime is a pressure situation, so the first thing you must do is try to release some of that pressure. Tell your team two things.

If you were supposed to blow the other people off the court but obviously haven't, tell your team that the opponent was underrated, has tremendously improved, whatever. Now, however, you are going to finish the job you came for. If you were underdogs, tell your team that when this one is over, you won't be taken lightly anymore. Either way, give them a little confidence builder.

Second, explain that you are now starting again. The regular game decided nothing. You have three minutes to go out there and get a decision. True, you aren't going out equal because of foul situations and the number of timeouts each team has, but look at it as if someone is giving you a second chance.

In coaching overtime games use a cautious approach. This is not the time to get cute or flashy. You have a reliable offense that gives you good rebounding position and shooting options. You have a defense with which you are most comfortable. Rarely does an overtime become a run-and-gun game. The first minute and a half go by quickly. Both teams should be looking for good, high percentage shots. This is not the time for a run down the floor and then pull up for a twenty-five foot jumper. Protect the ball bringing it down the court. Work the ball for a good shot. Try to work the ball to an area where a defender has four fouls. She still doesn't want to foul out and may ease up on defense, making the shot easier. When you work the ball into her area, check to see if one of her teammates is leaving her responsibility to come and help on defense. If this occurs, the next time you are on offense go back to the same area, trying to draw the second defender to the ball. Get the ball to the open player. That will be your key shot. If any opening to the basket exists, try to drive. Overtime is an excellent time for the three point play. Don't attempt it at the risk of a charge, however.

In Chapter 8 special situation plays were discussed. When you start the overtime, use your most successful jump-ball play; i.e., most successful against this opponent. Getting that first basket is a tremendously uplifting psychological factor. The out-of-bounds plays will also become a big factor in overtime. The defense tends to get pumped up and many more passes around the baseline seem to be slapped out of bounds. The special plays will pay off here. In our four overtime games over the past few years, the special plays have always made the difference. The first basket from the jump ball to open the final three minutes and the aggressiveness, to-the-basket-thinking, of our out-of-bounds plays brought us points while our opponents have been consistently satisfied with possession.

The first minute and a half of the overtime flies by. The second minute and a half seems like an eternity. If you have a lead at this juncture, stall. Take only a sure layup. If you are on the short end of the score, foul quickly. You must get the ball and that's the fastest way. Follow the same strategy as the final two minutes of regulation play in the preceding section, as far as fouling goes. Go for the ball, not the body. You must continue this strategy until you get a lead or a tie.

If you have a tie with a minute or less on the clock, use your stall until a clear shot is available. Remember if you are stalling, have your best ball handlers in the game even if it means playing four guards at one time. You are looking for a sure inside shot—preferably a layup. You don't need rebounding height in that situation.

If you lose an overtime game, make sure you analyze exactly why you lost. Almost every time there was one reason. Eliminate that reason next time. It may have been a player who didn't know a play; a player who didn't follow your directions, a player who quit on defense, a player who fouled out because you didn't protect her earlier in the game. It was some one factor that you must identify. Overtimes are seldom blowouts. They generally are nip-and-tuck battles that are won or lost because of a small factor. Be sure you identify what it is before your next game. It too could be a tie.

11

GETTING MOMENTUM
AND KEEPING IT

Every year at tournament time coaches are interviewed by the media and the majority at some point in the exchange discuss momentum. They talk about their slow start and the gradual development that has taken place over the season. They all want their teams to peak at the "right time" — tournament time. Yet if you look at the records of most teams, the facts don't support the statements. Teams have, in reality, bounced through the season with wins and losses. Games have been lost to teams of lesser ability. Games have been won over teams of greater ability. This does not reflect a steady upward climb. Rather, it shows an instability which is precisely what you want to avoid.

Take a look at the teams that have amassed a strong winning tradition over a period of years. They all have one thing in common: strong performance at the beginning of the season. It didn't come by coincidence. It was generated by the philosophy, confidence and ability of the coach. You have specific beliefs about what basketball is all about. You see a purpose in the game and you want to achieve that purpose. If you believe you need height to win and you have little or no height, your players are going to learn this quickly through your words and actions, and any chance for success fades just as quickly because of your lack of confidence. There are offenses and defenses that are successful for any combination of players. Your disappointment in the absence of height, speed, or quickness will be recognized by your players and they will adopt your attitude. It is imperative that you show confidence from the beginning in their ability, whatever it is.

Through years of observation and involvement I have come to the opinion that, just as in farming, there are years when athletics yields a bumper crop. A few years ago we had a team that went undefeated. At the end of the season, I told the team that if they had lost a game it would have been my fault. I was fortunate enough to get them. Other years have not been as plentiful in terms of talent, but you never let the team know that. At the beginning of the season you have a group of optimistic, eager young women. You grasp that attitude and build on it with your own optimism and enthusiasm.

It takes more than optimism and enthusiasm to be a winner, however. It takes skill and knowledge for both you and the players. Lesser skilled players can be successful if they can keep errors to absolute minimums and if they are taught the game. Therefore you should spend much of your preseason working on fundamentals and explaining the game. In those first games, stress your successes specifically in those areas. You can use whole games or just a quarter to show the team the relationship of their scoring or the lack of opponent scoring to turnovers. Talk about their strengths and successes. Praise all success. You know from your own experience how much effort will be put forth in hope of praise. And effort is what you are seeking because in the final analysis, most teams are fairly evenly matched and total effort is the deciding factor. Your confidence, which the team adopts, and praise will get you the needed effort to start your season strong.

A successful way to create momentum is to have a team motto. The personality of the group will determine to how great a degree you use the motto. A few years ago the Dixie-Marathon Company had a sales promotion and used the slogan "Good enough just isn't good enough." I was able to get buttons, which the company made, with this imprinted on them and gave one to each team member. Regardless of the opponent, we could use our rallying cry before each game. With another team, we simply used the word "yes." It kept us positive throughout the season. In other years, posters were placed in the gym at the beginning of the season. The quotes used came from motivational books from writers such as Napoleon Hill. At the proper times, we would refer to the posters. These are just a few of the ways you can motivate your team from the beginning of the season. Through their repeated use through the year you can keep momentum because the team feels a togetherness, a unit working with each other and for each other.

CREATING TEAM ATTITUDE AND RESPECT

Each of us wants to have a team that has a positive attitude, one that says we believe in ourselves and what we are doing. We also want to believe in each other and respect each other. Depending on your school system, we may or may not have an influence on the schools that are the feeder system for our program. If you are part of a large school district, the middle schools or junior high schools may be extraordinarily diverse in their athletic programs. Coaching tenure may be brief. Lower level coaches may have little or no training for the job. And certainly the personalities of the coaches will fall at every point on a continuum from soft-spoken and mild-mannered to boisterous and temperamental. Player personalities will vary as widely. The players have grown up in a multiplicity of environments that include loving, caring homes, uninvolved parents, argumentative parents or win-at-any-cost parents and coaches. The majority of the players care about their teammates and coaches. They participate with good sportsmanship in mind and they give total effort. They will listen to you and be team players. Your organizational meeting speech about team play must be strong. It must convince them that basketball is a team sport where every person's contribution is valuable—player, coach, trainer and manager.

Not all players are team players, however. There are some who, for whatever reason, are interested in themselves. They want to be stars. Their tantrums may work at home. Their parents may buy them anything they want but not give them love. As a result, they try any antics to get your attention. Their parents may have high expectations, beyond reality, and may be applying pressure for the athlete to achieve stardom at the team's expense. Respect is not in the player's vocabulary and selfishness is her attitude. She doesn't hear your speeches about team work because she doesn't want to hear them. She will be the player who, after a game, asks how many points she has scored. She is not interested in what other players did unless she is asking for comparison purposes. This is the player who will shoot when she's covered or before a play is developed. If you are fortunate you won't have one of these players on your team but it is likely that you will. The majority work well together, care about each other and try for the group. But the exception is the one who will give you and the team problems.

Your key in working with this individual is to be consistent in your behavior. Continue to praise success but relate it to team success. Praise her assist production more than her scoring. If she becomes a "gunner" during a game, take her out and explain what type of play is needed for the team's benefit. Put her in a situation where she sets the screens. Don't tell her that she is a gunner or berate her for selfishness. That's negative. Continue to praise for team play and put her in situations where she has to be a team player. Don't give her more attention than other players. That's what she wants and the other players will see what negative behavior gets. You may spend the season trying to change her negative selfish attitude, and you may fail but it is your job to create a good positive team stance.

TEAM RECOGNITION OF THE SEASON *VS.* A GAME

In most leagues or conferences, there always seem to be one or two teams that dominate for a short number of years.

Sometimes a school will always be near the top. As a result they become the team to beat. Sometimes coaches allow these teams to dominate their thinking and by spending too much practice time preparing for them, lesser skilled teams will pull upsets. The losses to lesser teams are usually mental and emotional defeats. Your job is to eliminate the mental and emotional peaks and valleys of a season by placing a game in perspective within a season.

You want to have a season that shows growth as individuals and as a team. That growth won't be achieved if you gear your team towards only a few select games. Each game is important, including nonconference games, if you want to set a base and continuously build on it. You begin with some basic offenses and defenses and through practices develop more complexity as the season progresses. You can't accomplish that progression if development is set aside for the sole purpose of defeating a specific opponent. Your team spends too much time worrying about the specific skills of the opponents' outstanding players. Team defense will stop those opponents, a defense that has been primed through continued practice.

It is impossible to keep all games of equal importance. Your girls want to knock off a league leader or an unbeaten team. To keep the game in perspective with others, however, you should form goals for that game. It takes the pressure off one player who is defending a star. The star may get her average, but if you can stifle the rest of the team, you will reach a defensive goal. Set an offensive goal for halftime so the team is deliberate in its offensive effort. Don't talk in terms of what the halftime score or game outcome is going to be. Just set goals for *your* team, realistic goals.

When you are scheduled to play a team that has a reputation for being weak, set a practice tone of the importance of good play. As trite as it may sound, don't take anyone for granted. Getting a team emotionally ready for the top team is relatively easy. Getting it ready for the bottom team is difficult. Here again specific goals are needed. Stressing a low turnover total is valuable. Tennis players often talk about playing at the level of their opponents. Against a weak or sloppy player, they tend to produce the same effort. Basketball teams often do the same thing. By setting a low turnover goal, you encourage clean, thinking, smooth basketball, and at the same time work to avoid the upset by assuming victory.

Your team should think of a basketball season as a ladder, with each game as a rung. Schedules are always printed with the first game on the top of the page working downward to the last game. The ladder approach can be achieved by making your own schedule for the gym or locker room. You write in each game as it comes starting at the bottom of the poster board, working your way to the top. In fact the influence of the schedule construction is even greater if a different player adds each game.

ALLOWING NO DISASTERS

Disaster can be defined in many ways. A thirty or forty point blowout in a game can be one definition. An eight or nine game losing streak can be another. A growing, festering sore spot among the players that explodes into dissension among the team members can be another. Losing two consecutive games if you are a conference leader and you are nearing the end of the season can even apply here. There are many ways to define the word and avoiding all disasters is the job of the coach, not of anyone else.

When you are in the second quarter of a game, you have a clear idea if the two teams are fairly evenly matched or if they are mismatched. If you find your team is down and the opponent has much greater skill, you still obviously try to win the game, but at the same time you want to avoid a lopsided score. If it is very early in the season and many of the players are returning from a losing season, a blowout game can be demoralizing enough to cause you to spend half of the season building the morale up again. Slow the game down to as deliberate a pace as possible. Keep working the ball for specific shots. It will reduce the amount of scoring for both sides, but by working for only certain high percentage shots, you can keep scoring—true, at a slow rate—but your opponents won't be scoring at will because they won't have the ball. Explain to your team at half time or during a timeout when you make the change that you want them to take only high percentage shots.

You may lose a series of games for the obvious reason that you have very little skill. However, unless you have the smallest enrollment in your conference and are always at the bottom in the standings (changing your conference, if possible, should be considered), you should win some of your games. Your problem may be that you are one dimensional in your approach either offensively, defensively, or both. If you have one zone offense and try to force it against man-to-man defense, you will have difficulty being successful. If you have only a zone defense and the opponents early in each game find the weaknesses and pick it apart, the losses will mount. Teach at least two offenses and two defenses in preseason so you have an alternative to change to should problems arise in a game. As the season progresses, add to them, modify them, sophisticate them. You stay simple enough to pursue excellence in what you do but you must have diversity in meeting different teams.

Another reason for losing a series of games is that you are using offenses and defenses that don't utilize your players' skills. If you like fast-break basketball, but you don't have players with the skills to play it, don't use it. If you think man-to-man is the panacea for all defensive problems, but you have no quickness and your defenders are always a step behind or fouling, you are just frustrating your team and losing games at the same time. One year I spent much of my free time in the spring and summer developing a weave offense. When the team was chosen, I couldn't wait to teach it to them. After one week of total frustration for me the players were no farther ahead on day five than they were on day one. The weave was junked and they learned the midpost and a simple rotation offense. The weave required a sense of floor balance. This team could shoot, dribble, pass and rebound, but floor balance they were missing. Had we kept the weave, they would have joined me in frustration, lost games and therefore lost morale because I wanted that offense. The simple rotation eventually taught them floor balance but not at the expense of a season. Forcing your pet offense or defense can be very expensive. It can cost you a season.

Sometimes a series of losses can result from an unhappy team. Usually it's only a few players but it can spread rapidly, causing bad feelings. The common cause of bad feelings is lack of playing time. No one likes to sit on the bench, but you can accept it if you know you will get to play or if a coach explains why your playing time is limited. When I was a first year player on a softball team and younger than most of the other players, our manager told me in clear words that I'd play very little. I had to practice to achieve the skill level of the rest of the team. When I was put in the game—right field in the seventh inning with a score of 19-0, I knew why. Substitutes want to know why they aren't starters and why they didn't get to play last night. They will accept explanation; they won't accept silence. Repeated nights on the bench with no participation causes many to start thinking practice isn't worth the effort. They go through the motions but don't give any real effort. The rest of the team soon realizes the problem. Unless you have a captain who keeps you informed, you may not realize the problem. Instead you keep working on motivational techniques to get the team to work hard. The problem is one of communication. Talk to your players.

Playing time for substitutes can be remedied rather easily. Taking a year off to do graduate work, I had the opportunity to be one of those hundred coaches in the stands. In the beginning of my coaching, I used to be a "three-quarter" coach. You play the starters and the sixth and seventh players for three and three-quarters, then you sub in the bench if you have a big lead or are down by an insurmountable amount. My year off gave me a chance to remove myself from the intensity of the game, and I watched some other three-quarter coaches. In game after game it became very apparent that the group on the end of the bench wasn't watching the game most of the time. It wasn't giving vocal support to its team on the floor. In watching these young women, I realized that they weren't growing as players and the teams weren't growing either. Experience has now taught me that you can substitute starting in the middle of the first quarter and play everyone.

The three reasons for not playing a girl are: she is injured, she doesn't know the plays, and she does not give total effort in practice. As long as girls are physically able and knowledgeable, and they contribute in practice, they should get in the game.

STAYING FRESH ALL SEASON

After three months of a basketball season have passed, you and the players tend to get practice-weary. The workouts seem stale; horseplay increases steadily. The problem is that practices have gotten too routine, too predictable. You may be using the same drills in the same order, you may be too methodical in game-by-game preparation for opponents. Whatever the reasons, the players begin to find reasons to be late, leave early or miss entirely. Coach, you're in a rut and the team's performance will reflect it. Staying fresh requires a variety of practices. Create strange, fascinating, funny practices. Ease the pressure and relieve the monotony that comes from repetition. Silly games may seem like a waste of time, but they keep the team alive, refreshed. It is just as important to be mentally ready for a game as it is to be physically ready. Emotions often play a bigger part than both of those factors. By changing your routine and using different drills you can keep your team emotionally healthy.

USING NEW DRILLS

To avoid boredom, change your environment or find new drills. Changing the gym is in most cases impossible but occasionally you can trade practice places with another team within your school system. Finding new drills, however, is easier and anyone can do it. You can make them up, find them in books or go to a valuable resource: the team. Most of our players attend summer camps from which they return with a wealth of ideas. Some of our most fun—and valuable—practices have been "Favorite Drill Days." Each player must bring in her favorite drill. Teaching the team and demonstrating is her responsibility. They have total freedom of choice. Any drill, whether it's one of ours, her creation or one from a camp, is acceptable.

Dribbling tag is fun and improves ball handling. Three players each have a ball, one is "it" and as each dribbles, she must tag another who is then "it." If the one who is "it" loses her dribble or double-dribbles while tagging another dribbling player, she is still "it." If one of those who is free commits a violation, then she is "it." The catch to the game: all three must stay in the lane area. If you step outside of the lane, you are "it." A wealth of laughter is accompanied by some terrific dribbling practice.

One player brought in the Mikan drill, named after the great George Mikan of DePaul University and the Minneapolis Lakers. You do continuous layups from alternate sides of the basket. You start on the right side of the basket standing still. You shoot a right-handed layup, get your rebound, take one step to the left side, shoot a left-handed layup, get your rebound, shoot a right-handed layup, etc. No dribbling is allowed. Each player is timed for thirty seconds; the player who makes the most layups is the winner.

Another player brought in a passing drill that took us ten minutes to figure out. It was worth it. Seven players are involved and it looks like this:

Row 1		2		1		3
Row 2	4		5		6		7

Numbers 1, 2 and 4 each hold a ball. On a signal they each pass the ball they hold. They can pass only to certain people. No. 1 passes to either 2 or 3. No. 2 passes to either 4 or 5. No. 4 passes only to No. 1. If 3 receives a pass from No. 1 she can pass to either 6 or 7. In other words, Row 2 always.passes to No. 1, No. 1 always to her right or left and 2 and 3 always to one of the two players in front of her. These are the passing routes:

Row 1

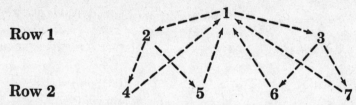

Row 2

You rotate left so each player gets to be No. 1, the "hot spot." When first learning the drill you soon realize that often all three balls end up at No. 1's place. The key to success is to keep a steady timing of the passes; i.e., work together. Along with the giggling when No. 1 gets bombarded with all three balls, peripheral vision, coordination, passing, receiving and teamwork are all improved.

You can also make regular drills competitive. The tapping drill against the backboard can be run with two groups. Divide the team into two halves. Each group lines up on each side of the basket at the same backboard for continuous tapping. The goal is ten consecutive taps against the board. On command the first player in each line throws the ball up to the board, the next girl puts it back up, and you keep this motion. If a girl catches the ball, if it hits the floor or if it goes in the basket, that team must start again. Teams count their taps aloud. The reward for the successful team is watching the losing team sprint a lap.

ADDING SHOOTING GAMES

At the beginning of the season, we end each practice with sprints and then free throws. However, as the season progresses, this becomes too routine. Therefore, we change to free-throw breaks and they vary. At any time during a practice, one girl is chosen to shoot a free throw. If she makes the shot, the team gets a water break. If she misses, the team runs a sprint.

Another free-throw game is to divide the team into two equal groups. The teams line up at opposite baskets. The goal is to make five consecutive free throws, shooting one each in rotation. The winning team gets to watch another sprint lap.

A fun shooting game is "Beat Annie Meyer." The name of the player can be changed to anyone in your area who is popular with your team. The rules of the game are that the shooter is allowed one free throw and one layup. All other shots must be taken from outside the lane. For each shot made the shooter gets one point; for each one missed "Annie" gets two points. The object is to get ten points before Annie does.

"Take Away" is also a good shooting game because it creates a pressure situation for the shooters. Divide a team into two equal groups. Each group member has a ball. Both are lined up at the same basket with one member from each team shooting alternately. Shoot, get your rebound, and go to the back of the line. You get one point for each shot you make. You take a point from your opponent if you make your shot and their shooter misses hers. For example, team A has three points, team B 2 points. A shooter from team A misses her shot but the next shooter on team B makes her shot. B gets 1 point for the basket and takes 1 from A because their player missed. Score: team A 2 pts; team B 4 pts. The team goal is five points. The loser sprints a lap.

Choose a spot on the floor. Each player takes five shots from that place. The shooter with the highest number of successful attempts gets a rest. Other players sprint a lap. Change the shooting spot each time you use this game to keep the advantage even among players.

In all of these games there is a competitiveness that keeps the players sharp, yet the games are varied enough to avoid a routine. You can also change the rewards from sprints only. Edible rewards are always a hit, and they don't have to be candy or soda. Oranges have great popularity among players, but cookies rated high with our team. We use sprints to add to their leg strength and avoid boredom of just running sprints. All of these activities relieve the dreariness that sets in after too many routine practices, practices that tend to be less and less productive, reducing team effectiveness. Keep the team fresh with new and varied activities. That freshness keeps momentum on your side as your team continues to be competitive and emotionally ready.

12

PLAYERS ARE
HUMAN BEINGS

While you prepare yourself technically to coach the game of basketball, you should also reflect upon your philosophy of the game and the role of each person involved in the game. All of the people in the game are just that—people, human beings—and all are subject to error. Further, each has her own personality.

Your job as a coach is to teach the game to each player as an individual and yet create a team—a cohesive, working unit. You cannot forget the individualism of each player, and yet when a person joins a group, any group, that person surrenders some of her individual freedom. For example, when joining a basketball team, each player knows she will wear the same uniform as her teammates. That is obvious. When she is playing the game, less obvious situations occur where she must surrender her individualism. If her main goal is to be the star and she shoots every time she gets the ball, her individual desire must be set aside for the benefit of the team. Fortunately, this example is the exception rather than the rule. However there are some basic thoughts about team play that differ in girls' basketball from boys!

In watching boys and girls play the same game I find an apparent difference in general player attitude. Our society

has taught boys to be leaders, girls to be followers. Even
though barriers are falling daily, occupations generally domi-
nated by one sex make the point clearer. Boys are lawyers,
doctors, principals; girls are secretaries, nurses, teachers. In
the former, we find decision-makers; in the latter we find
supportive, helping roles. In watching conference All-Star
games, the differences in attitude and philosophy is clear. The
boys take the ball to the hoop. The girls engage in excessive
passing. They seek peer approval in being a part of the group
which negates "hot dog" play even in a setting where it is
encouraged. It seems as if the girls prefer to blend in with the
group rather than stand out from the rest. In your own team,
you will find the same kind of thinking. It is a human
characteristic of the female that our society has created,
perpetuated, and rewarded. In elementary school, little boys'
boisterousness is attributed to the fact that that is how boys
act. Little girls who practice such behavior are called tomboys;
in other words they are not practicing acceptable and expected
little girl behavior. The girls learn quickly that the expected
behavior, if delivered, is rewarded by parents and teachers.
They are praised for being neat, clean, quiet, passive and
nonaggressive. We humans will go to great lengths to be
praised, therefore, girls are conditioned to conform to their
expected roles.

Many players on your team have been conditioned by
society to their passive roles, yet the fact that they have tried
out for the team shows that they want to be active. At the
same time, they believe that being too active will cause them
to lose their femininity. As a coach you should discuss this
situation early in the season. Participating in sports will not
cause you to lose your femininity. Those female athletes who
fill the sterotype "jock" image didn't have the characteristics
that society considers feminine before they entered the sports
world; there wasn't any so-called femininity to lose. Cite the
many examples of famous athletes who give one hundred
percent every time they participate and are still very feminine. Judy Rankin, Donna DeVarona, Chris Evert Lloyd, and
Wilma Rudolph are just a few. It is also helpful to name
athletes graduated from your school or program, girls with

whom your players are familiar. We have had many such players. One in particular stood out. As she sat in the stands during the junior varsity game, you would never guess she was the same player who would score fourteen points and haul down twenty rebounds in a game. Her beautiful locks would be tossed about, her face would be reddened from the constant running, and sweat would pour down her back. Yet after the game she came from the shower once again poised, attractive and beautifully attired. She was admired both for her athletic ability and her feminine demeanor.

While this beauty met the expected feminine role, you will also have some who do not meet the requirements. They still act and look like tomboys. Is it your job to change them? The answer depends on your philosophy. Remember that they have already surrendered individual rights in joining the team. It is important to show them that you think they have worth as human beings. Forcing them to wear dresses to the game (a requirement I have seen) isn't really going to change them. Respect their individualism even if it doesn't coincide with your beliefs. The only behavior that you should try to modify is one that is detrimental to the team's performance.

COACHES ARE HUMAN BEINGS

While sociey has expectations of the players, it also has made some unwritten requirements of coaches. As a coach you are the leader of the group so you, too, surrender some individual freedoms. The question is how many? Society expects you to be the model, the model for everything. I have known coaches in rural communities who were told not to be seen in the local taverns, although the townspeople who made the rule kept the bars profitable. Those double standards are found during a game also. Coaches can't discuss a call with an official during the game, but the people in the stands call the referee every unprintable name conceivable.

Society keeps one rule for men and one for women. Male coaches are credited with speaking up for their rights whenever they question a call. A woman is said to be a complainer, especially if she is a visiting coach (but then from the crowd's point of view, visiting coaches have few rights). The community keeps a scrutinizing eye on your attire too. How do you satisfy all of these expectations and still be your own person? Think of your players first. What is your role to them? That is where the lasting relationships are established, and those relationships are molded by your being honest with yourself and with them.

Trying to be something you are not results in the players seeing a lesson in hypocrisy. That's worse than their seeing whatever negative characteristics you have, and remember we all have them. We are human beings, we make mistakes and we hope we learn from them. The tolerance and understanding that our players have for that humanness is directly proportional to our tolerance and understanding for their weaknesses and failings.

KNOWING YOUR ROLE

While the coach's job is to teach the game of basketball to the players, it is more difficult than it sounds. Offenses and defenses can be learned at clinics and through reading. You can develop your own. But teaching them to a group of diverse players is the challenge. Simply because you have drawn them on a chalkboard and even walked through them on the floor doesn't guarantee that the players know or understand them.

When you are teaching individual offensive moves, be careful not to assume that because you can perform the move easily, everyone just learned it. The more simplified terms and steps that you can break any motor skill into, the more people will learn it. Take typing as an example. When you begin typing, you learn the letters of a particular finger and practice with that finger. You don't practice the entire keyboard all in the first day.

If you are teaching a post to receive the ball on the side of the lane and you want her to take the ball to the hoop, you explain that she takes two small steps with a low dribble, then she slides with a big step to the basket, pulls the other foot to the basket and drives the whole body to the basket.

Simply demonstrating the move, regardless of how perfectly you do it, is insufficient. Don't rely on your playing ability to be your sole means of teaching.

If teaching the game were the only aspect of the game, it would be an easy role. However, if you are coaching in a school, you often become a counselor too. You experience many emotional moments together with your players, and a player can come to trust you implicitly. She will tell you about a boyfriend, family members, friends, school situations. Sometimes there are problems with which she needs help; sometimes she just needs a listener. Good listeners are a rare breed; it is a skill in which we could all use improvement. Let your players know you are interested in them by being a good listener.

Also if you are coaching in a school, you should demonstrate an interest in academic achievement. Some of the players place a tremendous emphasis on sports, to which the classroom must take a back seat. If that is the path a player chooses to follow as a career, that's fine. But regardless of what college she attends, she must still pass basic courses in literature, social studies, math and science. The stronger her high-school background is in these areas, the easier her task will be in college. If you accept minimum achievement to have her remain academically eligible, you are doing her a disservice. One of the excellent lessons to be learned in sports is that you always strive to do your best. Ask your players about their classroom courses. Find out when tests and major assignments such as term paper are due. Stress the wise use of time to meet all of their requirements. In this sense, your role is one of making the players aware of responsibilities and of fulfilling them.

PRESENTING YOURSELF TO THE PLAYERS

In your preseason organizational meeting, your players form their first impression of you. They will walk away thinking the year is going to be much hard work or a barrel of laughs. You set the tone. Different players will interpret you in different ways, depending on their backgrounds, yet there is a general tone set. The returning players relate to the newcomers what your reputation is. If you are known for having high expectations, the girls will know that they must work hard in tryouts and practices. If you are low-key and easygoing, that also comes through to them. If you accept mediocrity, you get it. If you expect excellence, you get it. That's my thinking. It may not be yours. What is important is that you make your feelings known. Be you, not what someone else is or tries to be.

There are many coaching styles. It is possible to see some general categories, however. Some are organized, some disorganized; some very business-like, others the pal type. There are screamers, while the silent thinkers also exist. Each has been successful. You don't have to live up to an image. Your players want you to be you. The players can accept you as long as you are consistent. One coach I know is everyone's best buddy during practices and at games, yet she doesn't have time to say hello outside of the gym. That is very difficult for the girls to relate to. Whatever your personality is, keep it in all settings. It may not please all people, but we as humans can't do that. Coaches are no different. What is important is to be yourself at all times.

KEEPING EMOTIONS IN PERSPECTIVE

Because human beings, not programmed machines, are involved, sports are emotion-packed. We have all seen the extreme reaction in an athletic contest where emotions took over and an athlete or a team lost control, resulting in the inability to perform. Both anger at one's own failings and desire for revenge get in the way of concentration on performance. Your job as a coach is to try to avoid both.

In my first year of coaching, I allowed emotions to run unchecked during a game. After the game I realized what a fool I was. I also realized it contributed to our poor showing. Thereafter, I took a small plastic covered date book with me to every game. Inside of the flap in the front I placed a 3″ x 5″ index card with one word written on it: CONTROL. That word was printed in red letters large enough to cover the entire card; it sat right next to me on the bench during every game. After all, if I couldn't control me, how could I control the team? I still shout but now it's instruction or positive reinforcement. What is said now is worth listening to, not to be automatically blocked out.

While you as a coach experience many emotions during a season, your players will have just as many. Psychologists tell us it is healthy to express emotion. We see in boys' sports a stoical approach to the highs and lows of game actions and results. Girls tend to express their emotions more openly and freely. It is another aspect of coaching that you must deal with. Extremes should be avoided. No game that you win will change the world. No game you lose will end it.

When you win a game, you should be pleased if you played well, but even if it is your greatest performance ever and you overwhelmingly defeat your opponent, it is no reason to go berserk. Think of the other team. It has just lost and feels sad. Don't put salt in its wounds by going wild over a victory. If you are sharing a locker room, avoid screaming, yelling and locker-door slamming or pounding. Euphoric celebrating should be toned down not only in shared locker rooms but in a single one also. Your team can reach extreme highs only so many times during a season. Try to keep the emotions in check to avoid becoming emotionally drained.

Depression over losses should also be kept in moderation. Crying is a healthy release according to psychologists, however prolonged sobbing is unnecessary. No game is worth that extreme. My policy has been to tell the players that they are allowed one fifteen minute cry per loss. They are told with a half-joking manner. It is more important to resolve to come back strong through hard work in practice. Resolve to improve so you can avoid past errors.

A GAME IS A GAME IS A GAME

Games tend to bring out the best and the worst in us. For example, when an opponent is injured, I've seen two opposite reactions from coaches. One offered everything in the trainer's kit to provide aid and comfort to the injured player. The length of time it took to help the player in relieving her pain was irrevelant. On the other hand, a coach has grabbed the opportunity, calling her players together to give them instruction on offense/or defense. She also reminded the officials of elapsed time so the opponent was charged with a timeout because of the time used to tend to the injury. The former's behavior was commendable; the latter's was unacceptable. Did the second coach understand that it was a game? The well-being of the injured athlete is far more important than the outcome of any game. Yes, you want to win the game, but to what extent will you go to reach that goal?

Your behavior is contagious. Your players reflect your attitude and your actions. Can your players hold their heads high at the end of a season, knowing they can be proud of their efforts? Five years after their playing days are ended, can they say it was worthwhile and enjoyble? Former athletes of a coaching acquaintance reminisce about their playing days and invariably talk about the good times they shared. Their laughs are accompained by insight as they recall one particular game. The opposing coach will long be remembered for her comment, "Next time hit her so she doesn't get up," referring to one of our players. They sympathize with the substitutes who sat and watched as their team had a forty point lead with two and a half minutes to play and the starters still on the floor. Was it a game for them? Did the coach have her own definition for the word game? In the same game, towards the end, one of the starters sank a shot and raced to her defensive spot, shaking a fist in the air. It was easy to see where the attitude was acquired.

That fist was a good lesson, however, to the many people watching the game. The losing team could have adopted an attitude of revenge. They didn't. They had a philosophy that kept their perspective. They wanted badly to play the team again to show they were better players than they had shown that day. The opportunity never came and yet the feeling of "we can do better" prevailed in following games. They may not have been champions in title but, they were in stature. And isn't that what it's all about?

Playing basketball just for the sake of the game is losing

sight of the game's real significance. The games are almost scrimmages compared to the championship tilt called life. They are supposed to help prepare you for what is ahead.

At the same time you don't want to enter every contest with a lackadaisical attitude, not caring about the outcome. Your don't put in all of those long practice hours to go out to lose. You want to win the game, you want to succeed in life. That is why you work so hard preparing. If the team put forth its best effort but came up short on the scoreboard, it really didn't lose. All we can ever expect from the athletes is that they do their best. Their best is always "good enough."

PURSUING EXCELLENCE

For anyone to do her best requires hard work. Even if you have a losing season, if you and the players spend the season working hard to improve, you are successful. There is tremendous joy in seeing a player who has difficulty with some particular aspect of the game finally overcome the problem. We had one player who was intimidated when it came to driving the lane. After being turned away time after time by her own psychological road block, one night she went in for a shot up the middle and made it. The response was exhilarating. In the locker room after the game it was the only topic of conversation that seemed to count. The game score was irrelevant. She had made her move and had broken the ice. Her teammates were thrilled for her because they knew she had worked for it. The practice hours are physically, mentally and emotionally tiring. They are frustration-filled and yet they are what contribute largely to developing players as persons. They require dedication to improvement, not just to winning. If your players make a commitment to pursuing excellence, it is a quality they can carry through life. You can be their best example. As you spend a second and third season with the same team, you can show your commitment through increased learning. As you bring forth new ideas, drills and plays, your team will adopt the attitude of a willingness to expand and improve. As the season unfolds their best will continue to get even better as they pursue excellence, a goal each of us can have.

13

ENDING THE SEASON

After the last game, the season ends for the players. Many go on to spring sports. Some put their shoes away for a few months until summer comes when they work on their individual skills. Your season should also end. Regardless of how much you love the game, you should put it away for a brief period. If you coach other sports, you are forced to leave it. If it is the only sport you coach, give yourself a breather. That period allows you to return to the game fresh and view it as a game and not a continuation of the latest season. Before you file it away, however, there are some finalizing activities you should perform.

RECOGNIZING EVERYONE'S CONTRIBUTION

Each member of the team has contributed in her own way to the season. That contribution should be recognized. There are many ways to show your appreciation of their efforts. Your relationship with the team will determine how you want to show your gratitude.

Because of your stressing the game stats through the season, the players have an interest in their total performance for the season. Every team that I've coached has inquired into the possibility of receiving their individual statistics for the year. Just as with grades in classes, they compare them with each other, but they also look for improvement from one season to the next.

At the end of some seasons, the players received their individual stats with a personal letter that expressed my thanks for their participation and a statement of the player's strengths and weaknesses. Also included are suggestions on how the weaknesses can be improved. Besides the players, letters should be written to your unsung heroes, the manager and the trainer. They have performed valuable services, and they should not be taken for granted. Let them know you appreciate their help; give them a personal thank you. If your team has not been a closely knit group, the stats can be given at an appropriate time, such as a sports banquet, along with the athlete's school letter or emblem.

Another way of ending the season that a friend has used is the making of a scrapbook of the season. Clip all of the articles from the newspaper that have covered your team's games and paste them on plain white paper. Make photocopies of each page and assemble them chronologically in a booklet. Each player receives a copy of the memento.

Another friend has a team motto or quote that expresses the team goal or sentiment. The motto has served as a motivation throughout the season. When the year is ended she makes small posters with the motto on them and gives one to each member of the team. It's a nice touch that finalizes the season and symbolically says her thanks.

SUMMER PRACTICE WORKSHEET

Regardless of what approach you use to end your season, the players should be given an informal suggestion for summer work. Most players practice to some degree during the summer and many attend a camp to improve their skills. However, some work and can't take the time from their jobs. Others simply don't have the money to attend. The summer practice worksheet is devised to be used by any player regardless of position, financial status, and even motivation.

Each player receives a worksheet of drills to improve skills of ball handling, shooting and conditioning. The summer guide is written with the purpose of giving the player a number of choices of drills. It is also stressed that the drills are optional. There is no required work. Required summer work can be done with a negative attitude. Those who truly enjoy the game and who want to improve will practice, and the worksheet serves as an "idea source" for their practices. Forced summer work will not be a positive motivation. If you require the players to practice and use fear of not making the team, you can cause them to lose their enjoyment in the game. Come tryout time, it is easy to see who is in condition and who worked on improving her skills during the summer. You don't need any written proof.

The following is one of my summer drill worksheets. It is revised each year as I learn more, and for the benefit of the players who received last year's. New ideas help to motivate them.

IMPROVEMENT DRILLS

In using this drill sheet, be sure your injuries have healed. If you have any questionable conditioning or health problems that could arise from physical activity, CONSULT YOUR FAMILY PHYSICIAN BEFORE YOU BEGIN.

Choose those areas where you need the most work and always include free throws.

Warm up and stretch before doing any jumping to avoid muscle pulls. Don't work in hot, humid weather. It is too great a strain on your body.

Let your workouts be positive, fun times, not grueling negative work. This worksheet is to make you a better basketball player and that includes developing a positive, enjoying, competitive attitude and spirit. If you find there are drills that you cannot perform, don't be discouraged. Keep trying; eventually it all works out.

Good luck and have a good summer.

Shooting

1. 30 shots from each side of the floor in the 25°-50° angle
2. 30 shots from the high post
3. 15 hard driving layups from each side
4. 20 baseline shots—15' from the basket
5. 50 free throws
6. 15 running jump shots—several areas on the court (Driveway)

Ball Handling

1. Drive the baseline with and without a screen.
2. Change of pace dribbling.
3. Change of direction dribbling.
4. Lob, chest, bounce passes—strive to put the ball in a triple-threat position
5. Rebound, turn to the outside and release ball quickly.
6. Dribble hard to basket, stop quickly, head fake, jump shot.
7. Fill containers such as milk carton with sand, place them in a row or various patterns and dribble around them.

Conditioning

1. Jump rope for coordination and endurance in leg use.
2. Run—it's the best way to build your lung capacity
3. Increase your vertical jump
   a. do squats.
   b. calf raises.
   c. step ups on stairs.
   d. jump rope.
   e. keep a measurement of what the vertical jump is to see if it is increasing.

4. Shuffles—start with 2 minutes, increase 1 minute per week until you reach five minutes. Use the proper stance.

Specialty Skills

Rebounding: Tip the ball against the backboard. How many times can you do it consecutively? Remember to get position for rebounds, land with a wide base, get the ball quickly and safely to an outlet. Don't bring the ball down to your waist where someone can take it from you. Secure it.

Moves: Drive to baseline, reverse off the dribble for a jump shot.

Drive to side of lane, pivot, change hands for the dribble, give to middle of lane, head fake, jump shot.

Big players move—receive a pass on the side of the lane, 2 short dribble steps, slide in to the basket, power the ball up to the basket with your body, use backboard to drop the ball into the basket.

Playing with others: Get in as much one-on-one, two-on-two work as possible. It improves all of your skills because of the defensive contact, which requires greater concentration.

Note the many options that include the need for another player. Players tend to practice with teammates and their increased working together will help during the next season. They get to know each other's moves better. Also, no special equipment is needed. Even if the player doesn't have access to a gym or a hoop above the garage door, any of the work can be done at a public park. Finally, all of the drills have been used in our practices, other than the milk cartons, where we use cones instead. The girls are familiar with the drills and they know what the end result should be, therefore, they know when they are improving.

RECAPPING THE STATS FILE

In order to give the players their year-end statistics, you will have to recap the stats from all of the games. There is more than that single purpose in doing so, however. You can learn your defensive strengths and weaknesses by compiling shot charts of successful shots. Using a shot chart, place a dot for each successful shot made against you for the entire season. Having done this one year, I was amazed to find that the zone responsibility of the guard left of the basket in the key had only seven dots. That was for fifteen games! Two girls had primarily shared that responsibility over the season. Had the recap been done earlier, we could have overplayed the ball forcing the opponents into that area more often, and let the two super defenders do their job. The seasonal recap certainly told me who would be the prime defenders the next season.

Offensively, do the same thing with a shot chart. Of importance in offense is a balanced attack. You want to see dots all around the perimeter and in the lane. If the dots are out of balance you can make adjustments with your offenses for next year. If there are too may dots around the perimeter and few in the lane, you need to concentrate on creating situations for layups, such as clearing out against man-to-man or penetrating with a low post.

In looking at the total turnovers, decide what you consider acceptable. It depends on what your predominant offensive approach was. For a slow, deliberate offense an average of ten to twelve turnovers per game is realistic. However, if you rely on the fast break for your point production, you can expect a higher turnover rate. If you have a deliberate zone offense and average eighteen to twenty turnovers per game, your players need much more work in ballhandling drills.

One of the areas that often goes unnoticed is fouls. The one or two players that consistently foul out of the game are noticed, but how often do you study total team fouls? Your team may have many close games and if you've lost many by a few points, fouling may be the problem. Compare your total team fouls with the opponents' total. Are you fouling noticeably more than your opponents? In your practices next season, devote more time to reaction drills and foot work. Crossover steps put a player a step behind. Include shuffles or slide steps in your daily warm-ups. Reaction drills can help to keep a player even with an opponent who is moving, eliminating a desperation grab or lunge, which results in a foul.

Analyze each category of statistics and determine if they are satisfactory. Some will meet or exceed your expectations. Some will fall short. The latter are those that will affect your practices and plans for the following season. The former simply need the daily polishing time.

LEAVING A RECORD FOR THE FUTURE

Whether you are returning to the program next year or not, you want to leave as comprehensive a file as possible containing information regarding your team and your conference opponents. If you are returning, you have a ready reference of strengths and weaknesses upon which you can plan another season. If you are not returning, you can make a courteous, helpful gesture for your successor, who would otherwise be starting from scratch.

In compiling an information file about your regularly scheduled opponents, make a folder or index card (depending on how extensive a file you will build) for each team. That card should list key returning players. Include more than just high scorers. Make note of their best defenders. Describe the offenses and defenses the team used a majority of the time. If the team made drastic changes in the game such as moving from a zone defense to a full-court man-to-man in the last few minutes of the game, that fact should be included on the card. If the team was a conference contender but relied on five or six seniors, using its bench very little, you should also record this fact. That team may not be a contender the next year but may be rebuilding. If you won or lost to this team, explain what you thought was the deciding factor. Be as inclusive as possible, writing as if a person who knows nothing about the team were going to read it. That may well be the case. Imagine how appreciative you would be if you inherited such a file at a new coaching position.

In preparing a file on your team, you want to draw together all of the objective (stats) and subjective (your evaluation of skills) information for each player. Create a file that can be added to each year. In Chapter 2, an individual stats form is provided as an example. If you use this form, you can write your evaluation of the player's ballhandling, shooting, and defensive skills on the back or you can use a separate sheet of paper. For each year that the player participates, staple the forms together. In so doing, you have all of the information about the player consolidated in one package, rather than leaving the information separated in yearly files.

This information will be helpful to you and the player. At next year's tryouts you can judge whether she has improved upon the various skills. Further as women's basketball grows and develops, both the media and the colleges are paying more attention to the sport. If newspapers call for preseason information and prognoses about your team, you will have these consolidated files readily available. With more colleges providing athletic scholarships to women, your athletes are required to provide their statistical achievements. This is your chance to make that extra effort for a person who has given more than one hundred percent for you and the team.

When you have completed the files, your season has ended. The next one comes soon, but give yourself a break. It feels good to take some time away from the sport before you begin again to study the game by reading books and attending clinics. Take whatever time you need, but take some time. When you begin again to help yourself grow and develop as a coach, you will do it with freshness and vigor. Regardless of what has transpired in the last season, you have a new day dawning, an exciting beginning.

Index